Photoshop 5
Web Magic

Photoshop® 5
Web Magic

BY MICHAEL NINNESS

Photoshop 5 Web Magic

Copyright © 1998 by New Riders Publishing

International Standard Book Number: 1-56205-913-0

Library of Congress Catalog Card Number: 98-84902

Printed in the United States of America

First Printing: October, 1998

00   99   4   3   2

Trademarks

All terms mentioned in this book that are known to be trademarks or service marks have been appropriately capitalized. New Riders Publishing cannot attest to the accuracy of this information. Use of a term in this book should not be regarded as affecting the validity of any trademark or service mark.

Warning and Disclaimer

Every effort has been made to make this book as complete and as accurate as possible, but no warranty or fitness is implied. The information provided is on an "as is" basis. The authors and the publisher shall have neither liability or responsibility to any person or entity with respect to any loss or damages arising from the information contained in this book.

This book was produced digitally by Macmillan Computer Publishing and manufactured using computer-to-plate technology (a film-less process) by GAC/Shepard Poorman, Indianapolis, Indiana.

iv

Executive Editor
Beth Millett

Acquisitions Editor
Beth Millett

Development Editor
Beth Millett

Project Editors
Katie Purdum
Sara Bosin

Copy Editors
Sara Bosin
Christina Smith

Proofreader
Jennifer Earhart

Technical Editor
Kate Binder

Software Development Specialist
Craig Atkins

Interior Design
Gary Adair

Cover Design
Aren Howell

Layout Technicians
Michael Dietsch
Ayanna Lacey
Heather Miller

Contents at a Glance

Table of Contents

About the Author

Michael Ninness is a Senior Product Manager at Extensis Corporation of Portland, Oregon, a leading developer of productivity software for creative professionals. He is the former director of the computer graphics training division at Ivey Seright International, a professional photo and digital imaging lab in Seattle, and a former instructor for the University of Washington Extension's Certificate Programs in Computer Graphics and Photography. Michael is a regular speaker at the national Photoshop, Web Design, QuarkXPress and PageMaker Conferences produced by Thunder Lizard Productions, and has co-produced several Web Design seminars in Seattle and Portland.

Acknowledgements

Special Thanks to:

Vivienne—for all your support and encouragement, and for the subtle "motivation" reminders. Italy and France thank you too. Come over!

Beth Millett—"I'm almost done. No, really!" Thank you so much for the opportunity and the confidence in me that I could pull this off. I hope you are pleased with the results and that you feel your amazing patience has been rewarded.

Steve Broback—"I've known you longer than most of my friends." Doh! You have been my mentor and a true friend. Thank you for all your support and guidance over the last 10 years.

David Hoffman—Thank you for guiding a 23-year-old, arrogant young punk and providing me the opportunities that you did. For everyone at Ivey Seright, David is the best boss you will ever have.

C Dub—You're the greatest. Keep singing that song…

Thanks to my Thunder Lizard Productions colleagues: Steve Roth, Toby Malina (we MISS you!), Krista Carriero, Sondra Wells, Deke and Elizabeth McClelland, David Blatner, Olav Martin Kvern, Katrin Eisman, Greg Vander Houwen, Sandee Cohen, Rob Kerr, Ben Willmore and Jeff Schewe. You are all so amazing and inspiring to be around and I look forward to the next conference. (TLP produces the best Photoshop Conferences and other technology events around. Period. Visit them at www.thunderlizard.com)

Thanks to everyone at Extensis especially Kevin Hurst, Andrew Geibel, and Ted Alspach.

Thanks to Adobe for making Photoshop, the best imaging software on the planet.

Woo-hoo!

Dedication

for silly lady and sweet puppy. woof.

Tell Us What You Think!

As the reader of this book, *you* are our most important critic and commentator. We value your opinion and want to know what we're doing right, what we could do better, what areas you'd like to see us publish in, and any other words of wisdom you're willing to pass our way.

As the Executive Editor for the Web Graphics and Design team at Macmillan Computer Publishing, I welcome your comments. You can fax, email, or write me directly to let me know what you did or didn't like about this book—as well as what we can do to make our books stronger.

Please note that I cannot help you with technical problems related to the topic of this book, and that due to the high volume of mail I receive, I might not be able to reply to every message.

When you write, please be sure to include this book's title and author as well as your name and phone or fax number. I will carefully review your comments and share them with the author and editors who worked on the book.

Fax: 317-817-7070

E-mail: desktop_pub@mcp.com

Mail: Beth Millett
          Web Graphics and Design
          Macmillan Computer Publishing
          201 West 103rd Street
          Indianapolis, IN 46290 USA

Introduction

Mmmm...Photoshop.

Web publishing is getting easier and easier as the development applications are gradually catching up to their print predecessors. Even though we are now seeing an entirely new category of tools arriving on the scene aimed solely at the Web designer, Adobe Photoshop is still the king when it comes to working with pixels. Designing graphics for the Web doesn't have to be a big headache; in many cases, it can be quite liberating. After all, you don't have to care about CMYK or clipping paths! Woo-hoo!

The techniques illustrated in this book act as recipes for inspiring you to create killer Web graphics, while at the same time, helping you to discover new territory and features in Photoshop that you may never have realized were there.

You can quickly flip through the book and look at the thumb-tabs to see the results of each technique. Check out the CD for awesome demos and freeware from Extensis and other software companies.

Most of all, I hope you have fun and that the book helps you nail your concept.

Regards,

Michael Ninness

Before You Start

Welcome

This book was not meant to be an introductory guide to Photoshop or to the World Wide Web. However, even if you are new to Photoshop or creating Web graphics, you will still be able to find lots of useful information. Regardless of your level of experience, this book will help you build dynamic, show-stopping Web graphics with its easy-to-follow instructions. If you need an occasional reminder about a particular Photoshop command listed in a step, the Photoshop Basics section of this book will help refresh your memory on fundamental tasks without slowing you down.

System Setup

Most desktop computers now have plenty of power to run Photoshop. With each new Photoshop upgrade, there is an increase in the amount of memory that it takes to run it, but with so many computers equipped for multimedia these days, the basic requirements seem easy to meet. All of the effects in this book were quickly created on a 132Mhz machine with 64 megabytes of RAM and no special graphics acceleration.

When setting up your system, remember that you can never have too much RAM. Adobe recommends 24 to 32MB to run Photoshop. Allocate as much memory to Photoshop as you possibly can to get the most out of your machine.

It is not crucial, but it will help if you have a CD-ROM drive. A number of the effects in this book use files contained on the CD-ROM bundled with this book. (See Appendix B, "What's on the CD-ROM?," for information on accessing those files.) However, even if you don't have a CD-ROM drive, you still can perform most of the effects described in the book.

Adobe Photoshop 5.0

All of the techniques in this book were created with Adobe Photoshop 5.0, and that's the version I recommend you use. If you're attempting to duplicate these techniques using an earlier version of Photoshop, your results might differ slightly or significantly compared to mine. If you work with version 4.0, the biggest deficiency you face is the lack of the new layer effects features. I used these features in the book when they made things easier.

If you know your way around Photoshop, you can work around most of these situations. Almost all the effects can be created by version 3.0 also, but beware of the missing layer effects. In short, if you have an older version of Photoshop, you can use the techniques in this book as guidelines, but you might not be able to follow them verbatim. Most of the effects in this book use features that were not available in versions of Photoshop earlier than 3.0.

What's New in Adobe Photoshop 5.0

The latest version of Photoshop has many new changes. Some are minor and some are major. Two major new features change the way that you work through these techniques: layer effects and the History palette. The History palette is Photoshop's name for multiple undos. With the History palette, you can move backward and forward through up to your last 100 steps. Each of the steps appears on the History palette in the order that you performed them. This feature is invaluable when you work through step-by-step techniques such as those provided in this book. To return to a previous stage in the technique, all you have to do is click on the name of the command in the History palette. Or press (Command-Option-Z) [Control-Alt-Z] to move backward through the steps. To move forward again, press (Command-Shift-Z) [Control-Shift-Z].

Layer effects are features that enable you to apply built-in special effects to individual layers. Drop shadows, glows, and bevels are all covered by the layer effects. The interface for these effects is well-designed, making some of the techniques from my previous books obsolete. You can apply more than one effect to a single layer and even apply them to special type layers, also new to Photoshop 5.0, and still have editable text. It is important to remember that these effects are only applied to the layers. The information in the layer has not changed; the effects can be turned on and off at any time. These effects have been used in this book to save time and effort.

Conventions

All the effects in this book were created as 72 dpi RGB files because the primary destination for these graphics is a Web page viewed on a monitor. The dimensions vary from effect to effect—if specific dimensions are required, they will be noted in the step.

The Toolbox

For some of the effects, I used specially prepared preset files or additional software. Any of these extras files not included with the standard Photoshop software are listed in the Toolbox in the lower-left corner of the first page of each technique. The Toolbox lists everything that you need to create each type effect and any of its variations. The CD-ROM that comes with this book contains all the files needed to perform all the basic techniques. For information on accessing these files, turn to Appendix B, "What's on the CD-ROM?."

The Blue Type

As you work through the steps, you see phrases colored a light blue. These same phrases appear in alphabetical order in the Photoshop Basics section. If the phrase in blue asks you to perform a task that you are unfamiliar with, you can find that phrase in the Photoshop Basics section and follow the instructions on how to perform that task. Advanced users can perform the task as they normally would.

Menu Commands

You also will see instructions that look like this:

Filter>Blur>Gaussian Blur (2 pixels)

This example asks you to apply the Gaussian Blur filter. To perform this command, click on the Filter menu at the top of the screen and drag down to Blur. When Blur appears highlighted, a new menu opens to the right, from which you can choose Gaussian Blur.

In this example, a dialog box appears asking you for more information. All the settings that you need to perform each task appear in the text of the step. The preceding example tells you to enter 2 pixels as the Radius.

Click OK to blur the type.

Settings

Every step that requires a specific setting value will be noted in the step. Sometimes I will just give a suggestion and tell you to experiment with the settings on your own.

Photoshop 5 Web Magic

Tips

 Throughout the book, you will find additional bits of information that can help you render a better type effect. These tips provide information beyond the basic steps of each technique. ●

Photoshop Basics

The goal of this section is to help new and novice users of Photoshop with the basic tasks required to create the effects illustrated in this book. Each of the basic tasks in this section corresponds to the blue highlighted text in the chapters that follow. Here you can easily find the instructions you need for performing a particular Photoshop task.

This chapter assumes two things: that you are using Photoshop 5.0, and that you keep the Tool and Layer/Channel/Path palettes open. If one or both of the Tool and Layer/Channel/Path palettes are closed when you refer to this chapter, you can reopen them by name by using the Window menu at the top of the screen. If you use an earlier version of Photoshop, you can refer to the Photoshop manual for instructions on how to perform these tasks. Keep in mind that these instructions are for Photoshop 5.0 and instructions for earlier versions might differ.

The Tool Palette

If you're not familiar with Photoshop's Tool palette, don't panic. With a bit of experimentation, it doesn't take long to learn each tool's individual functions. To help the beginning Photoshop user along the way, here is a representation of the Tool palette. This also helps advanced users find the rearranged tools.

Photoshop 5 Web Magic

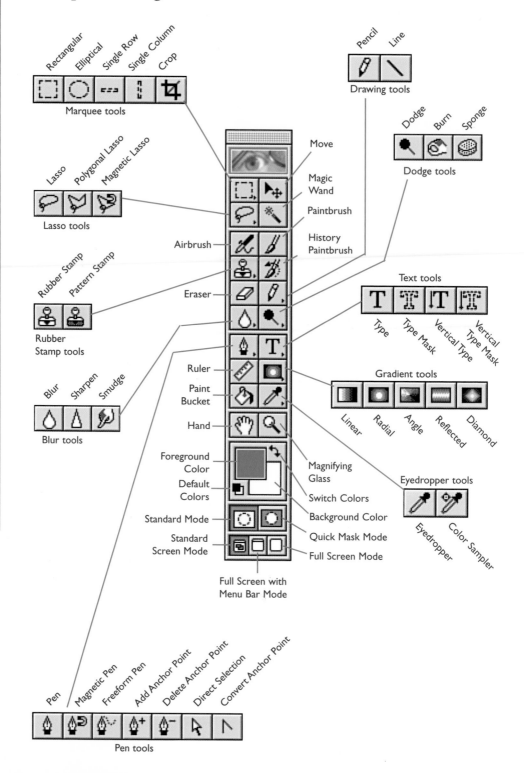

Marquee tools: Rectangular, Elliptical, Single Row, Single Column, Crop

Drawing tools: Pencil, Line

Dodge tools: Dodge, Burn, Sponge

Lasso tools: Lasso, Polygonal Lasso, Magnetic Lasso

Rubber Stamp tools: Rubber Stamp, Pattern Stamp

Blur tools: Blur, Sharpen, Smudge

Move
Magic Wand
Paintbrush
History Paintbrush
Airbrush
Eraser

Text tools: Type, Type Mask, Vertical Type, Vertical Type Mask

Ruler
Paint Bucket
Hand

Gradient tools: Linear, Radial, Angle, Reflected, Diamond

Foreground Color
Default Colors
Standard Mode
Standard Screen Mode

Magnifying Glass
Switch Colors
Background Color
Quick Mask Mode
Full Screen Mode

Eyedropper tools: Eyedropper, Color Sampler

Full Screen with Menu Bar Mode

Pen tools: Pen, Magnetic Pen, Freeform Pen, Add Anchor Point, Delete Anchor Point, Direct Selection, Convert Anchor Point

Basic Photoshop Tasks

Add Horizontal/Vertical Guides

Turn the rulers on (Cmd+R) [Ctrl+R], and choose View➡Show Guides (Cmd+;)
[Ctrl+;]. Click on the horizontal or vertical ruler, drag out a guide and let go of the
mouse after you have the guide positioned where you want it in the image. To remove a
guide, choose the Move tool and drag the guide back to the appropriate ruler.

Add a Layer Mask

Shortcut: Click the Add Layer Mask icon on the Layers palette.

To add a layer mask to a layer, choose Layer➡Add Layer Mask.

Adjust the Opacity of a Layer

Shortcut: With the Move tool selected, type any number on the keyboard or numeric
keypad to set the opacity of a layer in 10% increments. Type any combination of number
keys quickly to set the opacity of a layer in 1% increments. Press the 0 (zero) key to the
opacity of the layer to 100%. (such as pressing the 5 key sets the opacity to 50%, pressing 5 and 5 in quick succession sets the opacity to 55%).

To adjust the opacity of a layer, make the layer you want to adjust active by clicking on
its name, and then drag the Opacity slider in the Layers palette to the desired setting.
You can also double-click in the Opacity field and type in a value directly.

7

Choose a Foreground or Background Color

Shortcuts: Press D to change colors to their defaults: black for the Foreground and white for the Background.

Press X to switch the Foreground color with the Background color.

You can choose a foreground color from two palettes. Choose a foreground color from the Swatches palette by clicking on one of the swatches. To choose a background color from the Swatches palette, hold the (Option) [Alt] key while clicking on the swatch. Or choose a color from the Color palette by either using the sliders or entering numeric values. To enter the values using a specific color model such as CMYK, choose that model from the Color palette menu.

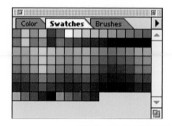 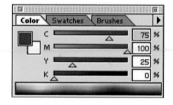

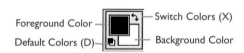

Foreground Color

Default Colors (D)

Switch Colors (X)

Background Color

To choose a Foreground or Background color using the Color Picker, click on either the Foreground color icon or the Background color icon on the Tool palette.

The Color Picker dialog box appears, offering two methods for choosing a color. To change the color that appears in the large area on the left, use the sliders on either side of the vertical spectrum. To select a color, click in the area on the left. You can also choose a color by entering numeric values. All of the colors I used in these techniques have been specified by their RGB values. Enter these values as percentages in the appropriate input boxes in the lower right.

Note that the Foreground and Background swatches on the Tool palette now reflect your color choices.

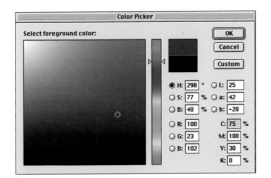

Create a New Channel

Shortcuts: Click the New Channel icon on the Channels palette. Hold the (Option) [Alt] key while clicking the New Channel icon to create a new channel and open the New Channel dialog box.

To create a new channel, choose New Channel from the Channels palette pop-up menu.

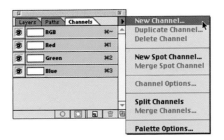

Use the New Channel dialog box to establish your settings. Unless noted otherwise, I used the default settings when creating a new channel. This figure shows Photoshop's default settings.

9

Create a New Document
Shortcuts: Press (Command-N) [Control-N].

To create a new file, choose File➡New. The New dialog box appears, which is where you name your new file and establish other settings. Almost all images in this book were begun by creating a file with these settings: Resolution: 72 pixels/inch, Mode: RGB Color, Contents: White. The Width and Height vary, but all values were set in pixels.

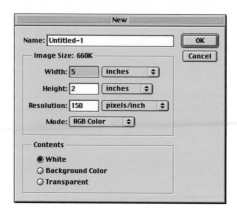

Create a New Layer
Shortcuts: Click the New Layer icon on the Layers palette. Hold the (Option) [Alt] key while clicking the New Layer icon to create a new layer and open the New Layer dialog box.

To create a new layer, choose New Layer from the Layers palette menu, or choose Layer➡New➡Layer. Or you can press (Command-Shift-N) [Control-Shift-N].

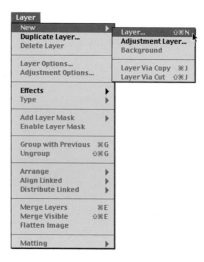

The New Layer dialog box opens, which is where you name the new layer and establish other settings.

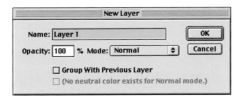

Create the Text

Photoshop 5.0 has four type tools. There is a standard Type tool, a Type Mask tool, and each of these tools has a counterpart tool that places type in vertical columns. In this book, I used only the standard Type tool.

The standard Type tool enters the type into a new layer. The color of the type defaults to the current foreground color, but you can also select the color by clicking on the color swatch in the Type dialog box.

This new layer is marked in the Layers palette by a "T" next to the layer preview on the Layers palette. If you want to edit the text, double-click the "T" to reopen the Type dialog box. These editable type layers can have layer effects (accessible from the Layers menu) applied to them and you can use the Transform tools on them, but you cannot use all of Photoshop's features to manipulate these layers. In order to do so, you must render the layer by choosing Layer➡Type➡Render Layer. After you apply this command, the "T" disappears from the Layers palette and you can no longer edit the type. The instructions direct you to apply this command when necessary.

To enter the text, select the Type tool and then click anywhere in the image to open the Type Tool dialog box. Type the text in the large box at the bottom of the dialog box, and make your attribute choices from the preceding options. Because many of the effects in this book apply effects that spread the type, you might find it desirable to increase the spacing between the letters of the words. To do this, enter a positive amount in the Tracking input box. Unless noted otherwise in the instructions, always make sure that you have the Anti-Aliased box checked.

After clicking OK, move the type into position with the Move (standard Type tool) or Marquee (Type Mask tool) tool.

11

Delete a Channel

To delete a channel, select the channel on the Channels palette and click on the Trash icon at the bottom of the palette. You can also drag it to the Trash icon (just as you would to get rid of a document on the Desktop by dragging it to the Trash or the Recycle Bin). Finally, you also can select the channel and choose Delete Channel from the Channels palette menu.

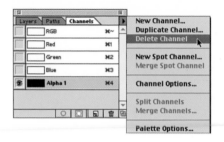

Delete a Layer

To delete a layer, select the layer on the Layers palette and click on the Trash icon at the bottom of the palette. You can also drag it to the Trash icon (just as you would to get rid of a document on the Desktop by dragging it to the Trash). Finally, you also can select the layer and choose Delete Layer from the Layers palette menu.

Deselect the Selection

Shortcut: Press (Command-D) [Control-D].

To deselect a selection, choose Select➡Deselect. The marquee disappears. If you have accidentally deselected a selection, you can choose Select➡Reselect to bring back the last active selection.

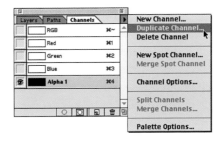

Duplicate a Channel

Shortcut: On the Channels palette, select the channel you want to duplicate and drag it on top of the New Channel icon. Hold the (Option) [Alt] key while dragging the channel to the New Channel icon to create a new channel and open the Duplicate Channel dialog box.

To create a duplicate of a channel, make the channel active and then select Duplicate Channel from the Channels palette menu.

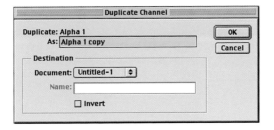

A new copy of the active channel is created automatically, and the Duplicate Channel dialog box appears.

13

Duplicate a Layer
To duplicate a layer, drag the layer to the New Layer icon in the Layers palette, or choose Layer➡Duplicate Layer.

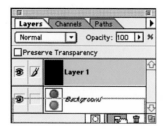

Exchange the Foreground and Background Colors
Shortcut: Press the X key.

To switch the foreground and background colors, click on the Switch Colors icon. This flips the two colors that are selected, and does not affect the image.

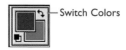

—Switch Colors

Fill the Selection
In this book, fill normally means to fill the selection with a color. To fill a selection with the foreground color, press (Option-Delete) [Alt-Backspace]. To fill the selection with the background color, press (Command-Delete) [Control- Backspace]. If you are in the Background layer or any layer that has the Preserve Transparency option turned on, you can press Delete to fill in the selection with the Background color.

You also can fill a selection by choosing Edit➡Fill or pressing Shift-Delete.

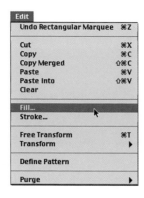

The Fill dialog box opens, allowing you several fill Contents choices as well as the ability to set the Opacity and Blending Mode.

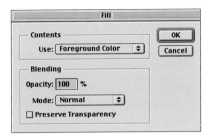

If the Preserve Transparency option is turned on for a layer, using any fill method only fills the areas of that layer already filled—transparent areas remain transparent. If a selection is empty (contains a transparent area of a layer) and the Preserve Transparency option is turned on for that layer, then you cannot fill the selection. To fill the selection, simply turn off the Preserve Transparency option before filling it.

Inverse the Selection
Shortcut: Press (Cmd+Shift+I) [Ctrl+Shift+I]

To inverse a selection, choose Select➡Inverse. This selects everything that is not currently selected and deselects what is currently selected.

Group/Ungroup a Layer
To group one layer with another, select the layer on top and press (Command-G) [Control-G] to group it with the layer below. Press Shift and (Command-G) [Control-G] to ungroup it.

Intersect the Selection
Shortcut: Hold down the Shift and (Option) [Alt] keys and click on the channel or layer that contains the selection to be intersected with the current selection.

Intersecting one selection with another selection results in a new selection that contains only areas that were part of both of the original selections. To do this, one selection needs to be active. Then either perform the previous shortcut or choose Select➡Load Selection to open the Load Selection dialog box. Choose the channel as the source and turn on the Intersect with Selection operation at the bottom. If you click on a layer as described in the shortcut method, the current selection intersects with the layer's transparency selection.

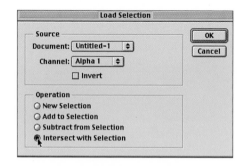

Link/Unlink Layers

To link one layer with another, make one of the layers active and click in the box that is just to the left of the other layer's preview. A small chain link icon appears in the box. To unlink the layer, click on the chain link icon.

Load a Selection

Shortcut: Hold down the (Command) [Control] key and click on the channel (on the Channels palette) that contains the selection you want to load. Or hold down (Command+Option) [Control+Alt] and type the number of the channel whose selection you want to load.

To load a selection, choose Select➡Load Selection. This opens the Load Selection dialog box where you can establish document, channel, and operation variables.

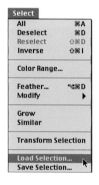
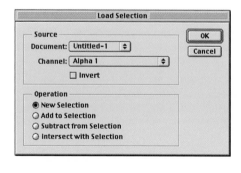

Load the Transparency Selection (of a Layer)

To load the transparency selection of a layer, hold down the (Command) [Control] key and click on the layer (on the Layers palette) that contains the transparency selection you want to load. The selection encompasses all nontransparent areas of that layer.

Make a Channel Active

To make a channel active for editing or modification, click on its thumbnail or name on the Channels palette. If you make the RGB channel (referred to as the composite channel in this book) active, all the color channels (Red, Green and Blue) become active.

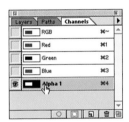

You can tell the channel is active if it is highlighted with a color.

Make a Channel Visible/Invisible

If you see an eye in the left-most column of the Channels palette next to a channel, that channel is visible. To make a channel visible, click in that column to turn on the eye icon. Click on the eye to remove it and make the channel invisible. If you make the RGB channel (referred to as the composite channel in this book) visible or invisible, all the color channels (Red, Green and Blue) become visible or invisible.

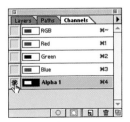

Make Guides Visible/Invisible
Shortcut: Press (Cmd+;) [Ctrl+;]

To make the guides visible/invisible, choose View➡Show/Hide Guides.

Make a Layer Active
To make a layer active, click on its thumbnail or title in the Layers palette.

You can tell the layer is active if it is highlighted with a color.

Make a Layer Visible/Invisible
If you see an eye in the left-most column of the Layers palette next to a layer, that layer is visible. To make a layer visible, click in that column to turn on the eye icon. Click on the eye to remove it and make the layer invisible.

Move a Layer
To move a layer, click on the layer you want to move in the Layers palette and drag it up or down the list of layers to the place you want to move it. As you drag the layer, the lines between the layers darken to indicate where the layer will fall if you let go. You can also use the keyboard to move layers. Press (Command-Option-]) [Control-Alt-]] to move the layer up one layer. Press (Command-Option-[) [Control-Alt-[] to move the layer down one layer.

The layer you moved appears between layers, numerically "out of order."

Nudge the Selection

To nudge, or move, a selection marquee, make sure you have a selection tool selected, such as the Lasso, Marquee or Magic Wand tool, then press the arrow keys on the keyboard the direction you wish to nudge the selection. Each press of the arrow key will move the selection a single pixel in the direction you choose. If you hold down the Shift key in addition to the arrow key, the selection will move 10 pixels.

To nudge actual pixels, (not just a selection marquee), select the Move tool first.

Rename a layer

To change the name of a layer, double-click on the name of the layer you wish to change to open the Layer Options dialog box. Edit the name of the layer in the Name field.

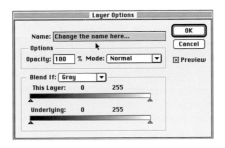

Repeat the Last Filter

Shortcut: Press (Cmd+F) [Ctrl+F]. To reopen the last filter's dialog box, press (Cmd+Option +F) [Ctrl+Alt+F]. To fade the last filter you used, press (Cmd+Shift +F) [Ctrl+Shift+F].

To repeat the last filter you used, choose the first menu item listed in the Filter menu.

Return to the Composite Channel
Shortcut: Press (Command-~) [Control-~].

If you want to return to the composite channel, click on its thumbnail or title (RGB, CMYK, Lab). The composite channel is always the one with (Command-~) [Control-~] after its title.

If you are in an RGB file, channels 0 through 3 are now active because each of the R, G, and B channels are individual parts of the RGB channel.

Save a Copy
Shortcut: Press (Cmd+Option+S) [Ctrl+Alt+S]. To do a Save As, press (Cmd+Shift+S) [Ctrl+Shift+S].

To save a copy of the file you are working on, choose File➡Save a Copy.

Save a File
Shortcut: Press (Command-Shift-S) [Control-Shift-S] to save a file with a new name, or press (Command-S) [Control-S] to save changes to the current file.

To save a file with a new name, choose File➡Save As. The Save As dialog box opens, in which you can name your new file and choose a format. To save changes to the current file, choose File➡Save.

File format selection depends on what you have in your file, what you want to keep when you save it, and what you're going to do with the file after it is saved. Consult a detailed Photoshop book, such as *Inside Adobe Photoshop 5.0*, for more guidance on which file format is best for your needs.

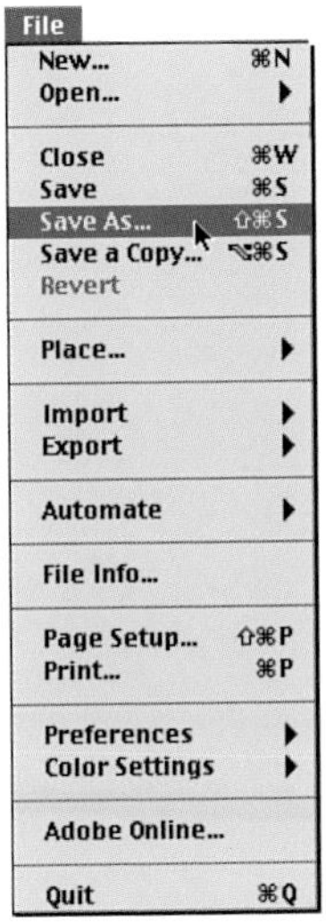

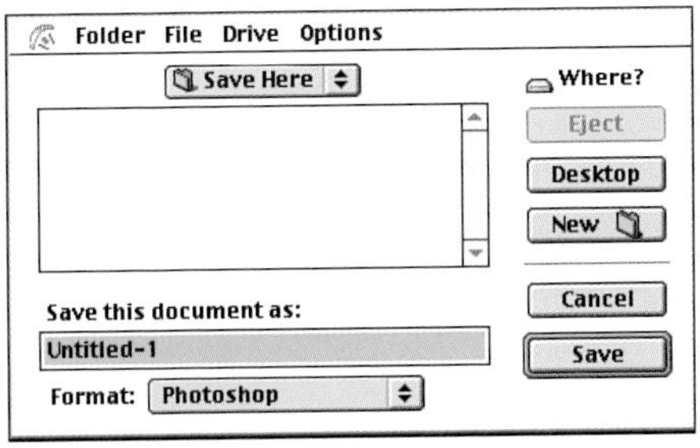

Save a Selection

Shortcut: Click the Save Selection icon on the Channels palette.

To save a selection, choose Select➡Save Selection.

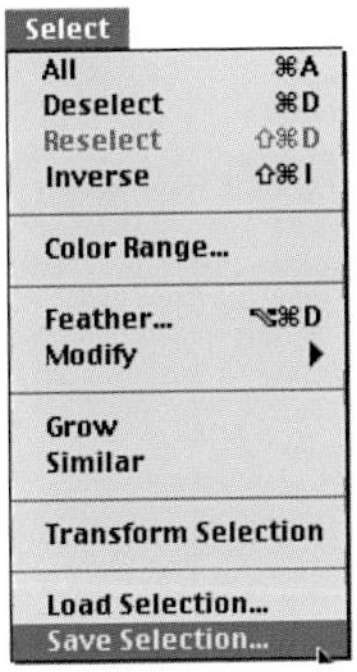

The Save Selection dialog box opens. Choose your options and click OK to save the selection.

Set a Layer's Blending Mode

Shortcut: Press Shift+(plus) to change the layer's blending mode to the next blending mode in the list, press Shift+(minus) for the previous blending mode. Press (Shift+Option+N) [Shift+Alt+N] to return a layer's blending mode back to Normal.

To change a layer's blending mode, click on the blending mode pop-up menu in the Layers palette and choose a blending mode from the list.

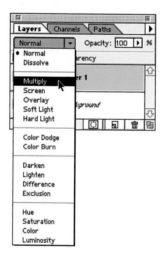

Subtract from the Selection

Shortcut: Hold down the (Option) [Alt] key and click on the channel or layer that contains the selection to be subtracted from the current selection.

Subtracting one selection from another selection results in a new selection that contains all areas of the original selection that are not part of the second selection. To do this, first make a selection. Then either perform the previous shortcut or choose Select➡Load Selection to open the Load Selection dialog box. Choose the channel as the source and turn on the Subtract from Selection operation at the bottom. If you click on a layer as described in the shortcut method, the layer's transparency selection will be subtracted from the current selection.

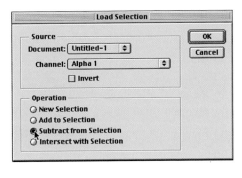

Switch to Default Colors

Shortcut: Press the D key to switch to the default foreground and background colors.

To change the foreground and background colors to black and white respectively, click on the Default Colors icon.

Default Colors

Turn On/Off Preserve Transparency

To turn on or off the Preserve Transparency option for a particular layer, first make that layer the active layer. Then click the Preserve Transparency check box on the Layers palette. This option is not available for the Background layer.

23

Turn On/Off the Rulers

Shortcut: Press (Cmd+R) [Ctrl+R].

To turn the rulers on, choose View➡Show Rulers.

Zoom

Shortcut: Press (Cmd+Opt+0) [Ctrl+Alt+0] to change the viewing percentage to 100%. Press (Cmd+plus) [Ctrl+plus] and (Cmd+minus) [Ctrl+minus] to increase and decrease the viewing percentage, respectively.

To zoom in on an image, select the Zoom tool by pressing the Z key and click where you want to zoom to in the image. To zoom out on an image, select the Zoom tool, hold down the (Option) [Alt] key and click where you want to zoom out in the image. ●

PART I

Animations

Animations are fun, but if over used, they can be annoying. This section attempts to inspire you by offering many different types of animations. Some of the most effective animations are very subtle—maybe only a small portion of the graphic actually moves.

Most of the animations illustrated here begin by creating source files of the images you want to animate as layered Photoshop documents. Then a separate product called Extensis PhotoAnimator will be used to animate the layers. An overview of PhotoAnimator is the first technique in this section and I recommend that you start there. All of the animation techniques have finished GIF files on the CD that you can preview in a Web browser to see the results.

All of the animation techniques in this book were created with the same workflow idea in mind: Create the animation source file in Photoshop as a layered document, save that artwork as a Photoshop file (.psd), then import that file and complete the animation in Extensis PhotoAnimator. This section will serve as a basic overview and intro-duction to PhotoAnimator.

Extensis PhotoAnimator is a stand-alone application and is available in both Macintosh and Windows ver-sions. A fully functional 30-day demo version can be found in the Software folder on the CD-ROM.

PhotoAnimator is a timeline-based animation tool. Unlike frame-by-frame animation programs, PhotoAnimator allows you to use layers and to apply effects to resiz-able cells. You can animate each layer independently and combine them however you like. You can edit your animation at any point and preview the animation at any time. PhotoAnimator also has multiple undo/redo just in case you make a mistake or change your mind about something.

Each animation layer can have mul-tiple cells, and each cell can have its own effect applied to it. PhotoAnimator automatically gen-erates the specified effect over a range of cell frames. You can easily expand or contract the number of frames in a cell, and PhotoAnimator will automatically recalculate the effect for the entire cell.

To create an animation, begin by creating your animation source file in Photoshop. Any elements that will remain static should be compiled onto the Background layer. All other elements that you want to animate should each be created on its own layer. If you name the layers appropriately, it will make things much easier later on because PhotoAnimator will import the layer names for you as well when you open the file in PhotoAnimator.

Now you simply open the source Photoshop file into PhotoAnimator. When it opens, PhotoAnimator will display the Photoshop Import Options dialog box. This dialog box gives you several choices about how to import your Photoshop files.

Layer Mapping Options:

The Horizontal Inline (frames) option will bring all of the Photoshop layers into PhotoAnimator on one layer. Each Photoshop layer will be converted into a single frame cell on this PhotoAnimator layer.

The Vertical Grouped (layers) option will bring each Photoshop layer into PhotoAnimator on its own layer and maintain the names of the layers as well.

Layer Import Direction:

From Top to Bottom, or Bottom to Top—this lets you decide the order in which you want the Photoshop layers to be arranged in your animation. What setting you choose depends completely on how you set up your Photoshop files. I typically arrange my layers in Photoshop from top to bottom.

Import Items:

This tells PhotoAnimator what items in the Photoshop file should be imported into PhotoAnimator. Most of the time you will only choose Layer Images from this list.

The PhotoAnimator interface consists of a single window, containing three separate panes: the Layers pane, the Preview pane, and the Filmstrip pane.

The **Layers pane** is located in the upper left of the window and displays all the layers available for the animation. Each layer can contain from 1–300 animation frames. This pane functions similarly to the Photoshop Layers palette, allowing you to create, name, hide, delete, and reposition layers. Most of these functions can be done directly in this pane using the buttons at the bottom of the pane, or by using menu commands and keyboard shortcuts.

The Preview pane, in the upper right of the window, displays a preview of the animation. This preview is always available and can be viewed from any dialog box as you work with animation effects. This is also where the Preview controls Play, Stop, Forward, Backward, and Loop are located (the buttons that look like those found on audio equipment).

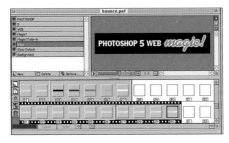

The bottom half of the window shows the **Filmstrip pane**, where you see all the cells and frames in the animation. Layers in this pane correspond to the layers in the Layers pane.

Layers, Cells, and Frames:
PhotoAnimator uses a timeline approach to animation. An animation can contain many layers, where each frame in the final exported animation is made up of the composite of all the layers for that particular frame, compiled from top to bottom—as if you were using sheets of acetate and stacking them on top of each other.

A single layer can contain more than one cell, and a cell can contain one or more frames. The number of frames in a cell can easily be modified by simply pressing and dragging the cell border to the desired number of frames. Each cell can only contain one image, so PhotoAnimator automatically repeats the contents of the cell in any new frames you create in the cell. As you will see illustrated in the animation, this perhaps is the best feature in PhotoAnimator.

For instance, if you want to have a logo move across a banner from left to right over 10 frames, simply select the cell that contains the logo, drag the cell border to the right until it contains 10 frames, then specify your start and end positions for the logo. If you decide that you want the logo to move across the banner in only 5 frames, resize the cell and PhotoAnimator automatically regenerates the effect for you over the new specified number of cells!

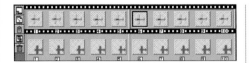

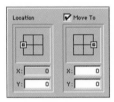

The active layer will display the black and white filmstrip border around it. The active cell will be highlighted by a red rectangle, and the active frame will be highlighted with a thick black border.

Moving

If you want the contents of a cell to move from one point to another over a desired number of frames, double-click on any frame in the cell you want to adjust. This will open up the Image Repeat Settings dialog box. Here you will see the Location start and end position controls. The grid on the left is for specifying the start position, and the grid on the right specifies the end position. Simply position the white rectangle on the grid where you want the image to be positioned in the frame. The X and Y fields allow you to enter an offset value (always in pixels). All offsets will start from wherever the little red rectangle is located. (For instance, if the red and white rectangles are positioned in the center of the location grid, and you enter in a value of 20 for the X and Y offsets, you would end up with the center of your image positioned 20 pixels down and right from the center of the frame. Using a negative value for X will position the image to the left and a negative value for Y will position the image down.)

These Location controls will also appear in many of the other dialog boxes in PhotoAnimator, such as the Image Scale Settings dialog box. Perhaps in addition to the image moving from left to right, you also want it to grow larger as it moves across the banner. Thus, you would need these Location controls in that effect dialog box as well.

Effects and Transitions

All other effects and transitions such as Scale, Rotate, Spin, Fade, Wipe, Barn Door, Gradient Mask, and so on can be found in the Effect menu. Select the cell you want to apply the effect to, then choose the effect you want from the Effect menu. Each effect will have its own respective dialog box with its own controls. Many of these effects are used in this book's animations.

Exporting

PhotoAnimator will automatically optimize your exported animated GIF for you. When you are ready to export the animation, select File→Export. This is when you specify what palette to use and how many colors should be in the palette, set the looping options for the animation, and so on.

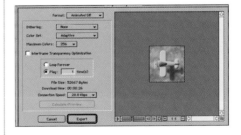

After you specify the export parameters, click the Calculate/Preview button and PhotoAnimator will generate a preview of the animation based on the export settings for you. It will also display the file size of the animation and estimate its download time based on the connection speed. Feel free to change the settings and click the

31

Calculate/Preview button again to compare the differences.

Once you have generated a preview, PhotoAnimator will remember those settings. As an example, you could choose 32 colors, generate the preview, choose 16 colors, generate the preview, and then switch back and forth between 16 and 32 colors without having to regenerate the preview. You can even compare different settings while the preview is playing!

OK. Enough overview. Go make some animations and have some fun! Try any of the animation techniques that follow to get started and then venture off on your own once you've learned the secrets behind the magic. ●

Animated Airplane

TOOLBOX

PhotoAnimator 1.0

plane-start.psd

In this animation technique, the background appears to scroll endlessly. To do this, you are going to create an animation of an airplane flying over a cloudy sky. The three elements in this animation are an airplane, the airplane's shadow, and a cloudy sky. Bring them into PhotoAnimator for a little work and presto!

Creating the Cloudy Sky Tile

1 Create a new document (500 × 500). Switch to default colors. Choose a blue foreground color (RGB: 102, 102, 204).

2 Choose Filter➡Render➡Clouds. If you do not like the particular clouds the filter created, keep applying the filter again (Cmd+F) [Ctrl+F] until you see something you like.

3 Choose Image➡Image Size. Change the Pixel Dimensions to 100 × 100 and make sure that the Resample Image checkbox is turned on. By scaling the larger image down to 100 × 100 pixels, you create an appropriately sized tile that you can use to generate the seamless background you need for the animation.

4 Select All and choose Edit➡Define Pattern to copy this tile to the Clipboard as a pattern. Close the clouds document, saving it if you want to use it for other projects.

5 Open the "plane_start.psd" file from the Artwork folder on the CD-ROM. You will see that the file is made up of three layers (Airplane, Shadow, Clouds). The airplane and shadow have already been created for you. The Clouds layer is empty, waiting for you to put the texture into it.

6 Make the Clouds layer active and choose Edit➡Fill (Shift+Delete) [Shift+Backspace]. Use Pattern for the Contents. Choose File➡Save As and name the file "plane_final.psd." Then close the file.

Creating the Animation

7 Open PhotoAnimator. (When the program launches, click the Demo button. By default, the New Animation dialog box appears. Click the Cancel button.) Choose File➡Open, locate the source file (plane_final.psd) you created in the previous steps, and click the Open button.

In the Photoshop Import Options dialog box that appears, choose Vertical Grouped (layers) for the Layer Mapping Options and Top to Bottom for the Layer Import Direction. Make sure that only Layer Images is checked for the Import Items and click the Import button. This brings the three Photoshop layers into PhotoAnimator as three separate layers, each containing one cell. Notice that the layers are named the same as they were in Photoshop. Choose File➡Save and name the file "plane.paf."

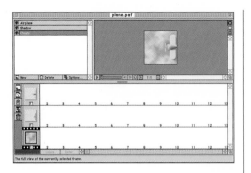

8 Choose Animation➡Frame Size (Width: 100, Height: 100) and PhotoAnimator matches the dimensions of the original Photoshop file that you imported. In order for the clouds to scroll endlessly and seamlessly, the original Photoshop file needs to be twice as wide as the viewable area. Next we'll position the elements within their cells.

9 Double-click the thumbnail of the airplane in the first row of the Filmstrip Pane. This opens the Image Repeat Settings dialog box. The location grids allow you to specify where you want the frame contents to be positioned. Click in the center of the Location grid on the left to position the airplane in the center of the frame. Change the values for X and Y to 0 (zero).

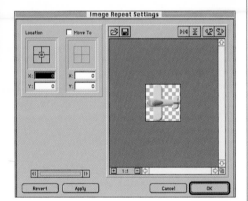

10 Double-click the thumbnail of the shadow in the second row of the Filmstrip Pane. Click in the center of the Location grid on the left to position the shadow in the center of the frame. Change the values for X and Y to 15 to slightly offset the shadow from the airplane.

11 Double-click the thumbnail of the clouds in the third row of the Filmstrip Pane. In the Location grid on the left, click the middle-left edge. Make sure the X and Y values are set to zero. Turn on the Move To checkbox. In the right Location grid, click the middle-right edge. Make sure the X and Y values are set to zero. PhotoAnimator moves the clouds from left to right starting at the left edge of the frame over to the right edge of the frame.

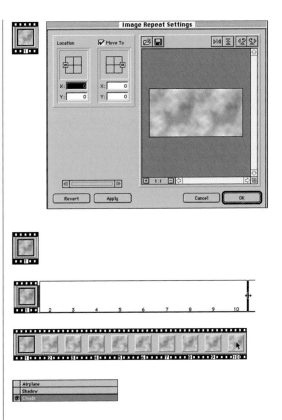

12 On the Clouds layer in the Filmstrip pane, position the cursor on the right edge of the cell border. When the cursor changes to a double arrow, drag this border out just past the Frame position numbered "10." This extends the background across these 10 frames.

13 Hide the Airplane and Shadow layers by clicking the eye to the left of the layer names.

14 Click the Loop Playback button in the Preview pane. Click the Play button or tap the Spacebar to play the animation. The clouds scroll by in a continuous, seamless loop.

Click the Stop button (the red square) or tap the Spacebar again to stop the animation.

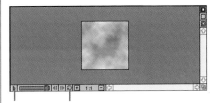

Play Loop Playback

15 Unhide the Airplane and Shadow layers. Select the Airplane layer by clicking it either in the Layers Pane or the Filmstrip Pane. In the Filmstrip Pane, extend the airplane cell to 10 frames. Repeat this process for the shadow cell, expanding it to 10 frames as well. Preview the animation. The airplane now appears to be flying over the cloudy sky.

Not bad so far, but to add interest, we will make the airplane bounce up and down as it flies through the air, as if the airplane were encountering some turbulence. Adjusting the scale of the airplane and its shadow over time makes the airplane appear to rise and fall. The airplane's shadow appears to shrink as the airplane rises and appears to grow as the airplane falls, mimicking a real shadow.

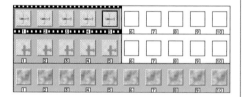

16 Resize both the airplane and shadow cells so that they each contain five frames instead of 10.

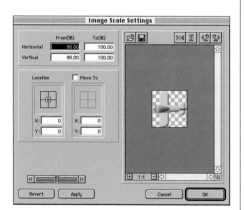

17 Click any one of the frames in the cell of the Airplane layer. Choose Effect➡Image➡Scale. Change the Horizontal and Vertical From(%) values to 90% and leave the To(%) values at 100%. This tells PhotoAnimator to scale the airplane from 90% to 100% over five frames.

18 Copy (Cmd+C) [Ctrl+C] and paste (Cmd+V) [Ctrl+V]. This creates a duplicate of the five-frame airplane cell to the right of the original. You now have two cells on the Airplane layer, each containing five frames.

Double-click any frame of the second cell in the Airplane layer. This opens the Image Scale Settings dialog box.

Change the Horizontal and Vertical From(%) values to 100%. Change the Horizontal and Vertical To (%) values to 90%. This completes the effect of the airplane growing larger and then smaller again across a total of 10 frames.

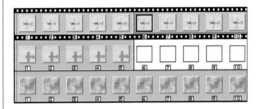

19 Click any one of the frames in the cell of the Shadow layer. Choose Effect➠Image➠Scale. Set the Horizontal and Vertical From (%) values to 100%. Set the To(%) Horizontal and Vertical values to 80% and click the OK button.

20 Copy (Cmd+C) [Ctrl+C] and Paste (Cmd+V) [Ctrl+V]. This creates a duplicate of the five-frame shadow cells to the right of the original. You now have two cells on the Shadow layer, each containing five frames.

21 Double-click any frame of the second cell in the Shadow layer. This opens the Image Scale Settings dialog box.

Change the Horizontal and Vertical From(%) values to 80%. Change the Horizontal and Vertical To(%) values to 100%. This completes the effect of the shadow growing smaller and then larger again across a total of 10 frames.

Tap the Spacebar to preview the animation. All that's left to do is to choose File➡Export and set the parameters of the animated GIF file.

You can view this animation by opening the "airplane.htm" file located in the Animations folder on the CD-ROM in a Web browser, such as Netscape Navigator or Microsoft Internet Explorer. ●

Complex animations look great, but often weigh in with large file sizes. How do you create really cool animation effects and keep the file sizes manageable? One way is to reduce the number of frames in the animation. For example, if you are moving a logo or a piece of type across a banner, the overall effect might look believable if you move it across 8 frames instead of 16. Generally speaking, the fewer the frames in an animation, the smaller the file size will be.

Let's take this concept one step further. Say you had reduced a 16 frame transition to 8 frames and have 2 end frames with the movement occurring over the 6 in-between frames. You may be able to replace those 6 in-between frames with a single frame that has been blurred.

This technique is effective because the human eye associates a blurred object with movement.

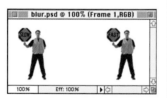

1 Open the blur.psd file from the Artwork folder on the CD-ROM. In this example, the first frame (the Frame 1 layer) of the animation will contain a man standing on the left side of the animation holding a sign that reads SLOW. The final frame (the Frame 3 layer) has the man on the right side of the animation, and the sign now reads FAST. Each frame has been set up as a separate layer in Photoshop with a white Background layer.

2 To make the single in-between frame, duplicate the Frame 1 layer and rename it Frame 2.

3 Select the Move tool and reposition the contents of the Frame 2 layer in the center of the animation. If you hold down the Shift key as you click and drag to the right, the image will stay aligned on its horizontal axis.

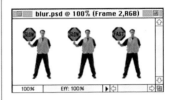

4 Choose Filter➡Blur➡Motion Blur. The Angle you choose determines the direction the object will be moving to and fro. The Distance you choose determines how fast the perception of movement will be. For this example, I used an Angle of 0 (zero) and a Distance of 40.

5 All that is left to do now is to export each layer out of Photoshop as a GIF file and compile them in your favorite GIF animation program to set the frame rates. Alternatively, you can save your animation source file as a layered Photoshop (.psd) file and import that into PhotoAnimator. More information can be obtained about PhotoAnimator throughout the rest of this animation section.

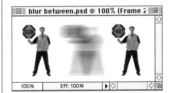

You can view this animation by opening the blur.htm file located in the Animations folder on the CD-ROM in a Web browser such as Netscape Navigator or Microsoft Internet Explorer. ●

In this banner ad animation, text is bouncing, zooming, scrolling, and fading all over the place! This complex animation is quite simple to create and after you get the hang of it, you can break apart the individual effects and apply them to your own animations. For this technique I have already created the source file and recommend that you use this file to learn how to make the animated effects described in the steps.

For this technique I want the word PHOTOSHOP to move from the right side of the banner, smash up against the left side, and bounce back into its final position. While this is happening, the number 5 should be scaling down from off-screen to its final size and position. Then, the word WEB must move from the top of the banner to its final position while the word *magic!* fades into view. It's simple, right?

1 Open the bounce.psd file from the Artwork folder on the CD-ROM in Photoshop to see how this source file is built.

Here are some notes about the bounce animation source file and strategies that you should apply to the files you will create on your own:

Create the Photoshop document at the actual frame size you want your animation to be. In this example, the animation is 350 × 60 pixels.

You can see that I made the number 5 much larger than it will actually be in the final frame of the animation. It is always better to work with a larger image and scale it down than to start with a small image and scale it up. All of the other elements in the file are created on their own layers and, very important are positioned in respective layers where I want them to appear in the final frame of the animation. All we need to do now is open this layered Photoshop document and animate it with PhotoAnimator.

2 Open PhotoAnimator. (Click the Demo button. The New Animation dialog box will appear. Click the Cancel button.) Choose File➡Open. Open the bounce.psd source file from the Animations folder on the CD-ROM. In the Photoshop Import Options dialog box that appears, choose Vertical Grouped (layers) for the Layer Mapping Options and Top to Bottom for the Layer Import Direction.

3 PhotoAnimator imports all the Photoshop layers to their own layers. Click on the Glow layer in the Layers list. Choose Animation➡New Layer (Cmd+L) [Ctrl+L] and name it Magic Fade-In. You will create a transition on this layer later on that fades the word *magic!* into the animation.

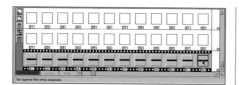

The layered film strip sequences.

4 Hide all the layers except for the Background layer by clicking on the eye to the left of each layer name. Make the Background layer active. Select Animation→Resize Cell (Number of Frames: 32). The animation will consist of a total of 32 frames. You just extended the black background across the entire animation.

5 Make the PHOTOSHOP layer active. Choose Animation→Resize Cell (Number of Frames: 6). Double-click on Frame 1 to open the Image Repeat Settings dialog box. PhotoAnimator imports the exact positions of the layered elements. The final position of the word PHOTOSHOP in the animation will have its upper left corner 11 pixels right and 21 pixels down from the upper left hand corner of the frame canvas.

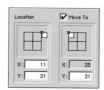

For the first six frames of the animation, we want the word PHOTOSHOP to move from off canvas, starting from the right side, over to the left side of the canvas. To do so, move the white rectangle proxy so that its upper left corner is aligned to the upper right corner of the start Location grid. Turn on the Move To check box and only change the X value under it to 25, leaving the end Location grid set to its default values.

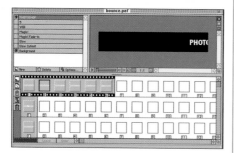

6 Copy and paste to place a duplicate of the cell that contains Frames 1 through 6 to the right of it. Choose Effect➤Image➤Scale. Turn off the Move To check box and move the white rectangle proxy so that its upper left corner is aligned with the upper left corner of the start Location grid. Next, change the Horizontal To(%) value to 40%. Leave all the other Horizontal and Vertical values set to 100%. By only scaling the horizontal axis, the word PHOTOSHOP will smash up against the left side of the banner across Frames 7 through 12.

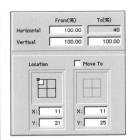

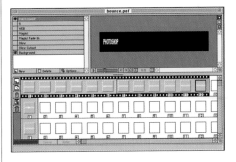

7 Copy and paste to place a duplicate of the cell that contains Frames 7 through 12 to the right of it. Double-click on Frame 13 to open the Image Scale Settings dialog box. Change the Horizontal From(%) value from 100% to 40%, and change the Horizontal To(%) from 40% to 100%. This returns the word PHOTOSHOP to its original proportions and to its final position in the animation across Frames 13 through 18.

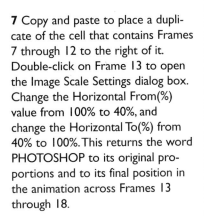

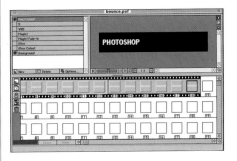

8 Copy and paste to place a duplicate of the cell that contains Frames 13 through 18 to the right of it. Choose Animation➤Resize Cell (Number of Frames: 14). Choose Effect➤Image➤Repeat and click OK to accept the defaults. This makes the word PHOTOSHOP appear in its final position for the rest of the animation. You have finished animating the PHOTOSHOP layer and can preview the animation—just tap the Spacebar once to do so.

47

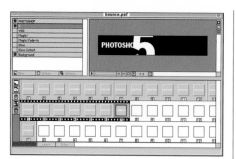

9 Make layer 5 active and visible. Choose Animation➤New Cell (Cmd+K) [Ctrl+K]. PhotoAnimator always creates and pastes new cells to the right of the active cell. Click on Frame 2 and drag it to the left of Frame 1 to exchange their positions. Choose Animation➤Resize Cell (Number of Frames: 6). Creating this cell for the first 6 frames hides the 5 until the seventh frame.

10 Click on Frame 7 and choose Animation➤Resize Cell (Number of Frames: 10). Choose Effect➤Image➤Scale. Change the Horizontal To(%) and Vertical To(%) values to 18%. Change the Location values to X: 136 and Y: 20. This makes the number 5 scale from large to small and positions it exactly where we want it, just to the right of the word PHOTOSHOP, across Frames 7 through 16.

	From(%)	To(%)
Horizontal	100.00	18.00
Vertical	100.00	18.00

Location   ☐ Move To

X: 136   X: 0
Y: 20   Y: 0

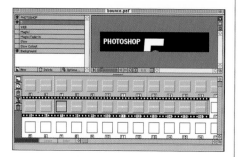

	From(%)	To(%)
Horizontal	18.00	18.00
Vertical	18.00	18.00

11 Copy and paste to place a duplicate of the cell that contains Frames 7 through 16 to the right of it. Double-click on Frame 17 to open the Image Scale Settings dialog box. Change the Horizontal From(%) and Vertical From(%) values to 18%. This makes the number 5 appear in its final position and size for the rest of the animation. You have finished animating the 5 layer and can preview the animation—just tap the Spacebar once to do so.

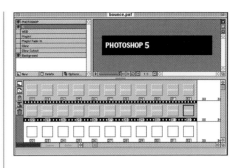

12 Make the WEB layer active and visible. Press the Home key to return to Frame 1 on the active (WEB) layer. Choose Animation➡ New Cell (Cmd+K) [Ctrl+K]. We don't want to begin seeing the word WEB until Frame 19, so move this new blank cell to the left of Frame 1 and choose Animation➡Resize Cell (Number of Frames: 18).

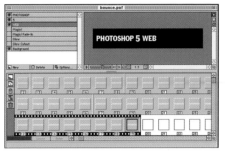

13 Click on Frame 19 and choose Animation➡Resize Cell (Number of Frames: 8). Double-click on Frame 19 to open the Image Repeat Settings dialog box. To set the start position, move the white rectangle proxy so that its lower left corner is aligned to the upper left corner of the start Location grid, and change the start X value to 157 and the Y value to 0. Turn on the Move To check box. To set the end position, move the white rectangle proxy so that its upper left corner is aligned to the upper left corner of the end Location grid, and change the end X value to 157 and the Y value to 21.

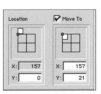

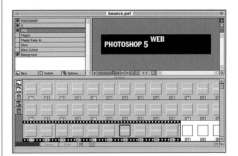

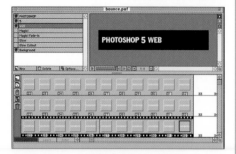

14 Copy and paste to place a duplicate of the cell that contains Frames 19 through 26 to the right of it. Choose Animation➔Resize Cell (Number of Frames: 6). Double-click on Frame 27 to open the Image Repeat Settings dialog box. Turn off the Move To check box. Move the white rectangle proxy so that its upper left corner is aligned to the upper left corner of the start Location grid. Make sure the X value is set to 157 and the Y value is set to 21.

This finishes the WEB layer.

15 Make the *magic!* layer active and visible. Press the Home key to take you back to Frame 1 on the active (*magic!*) layer. Choose Animation➔New Cell (Cmd+K) [Ctrl+K]. We don't want to begin seeing the word *magic!* until Frame 23, so move this new blank cell to the left of Frame 1 and choose Animation➔Resize Cell (Number of Frames: 22). Click on Frame 23 and choose Animation➔Resize Cell (Number of Frames: 8). You have finished animating the *magic!* layer.

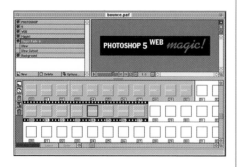

16 Make the *magic!* Fade-In layer active and visible. Press the Home key to take you back to Frame 1 on the active (*magic!* Fade-In) layer. Choose Animation➔New Cell (Cmd+K) [Ctrl+K]. We don't want to begin seeing the word *magic!* fade into view until Frame 23, so choose Animation➔Resize Cell (Number of Frames: 22). Choose Animation➔New Cell (Cmd+K) [Ctrl+K]. Click on Frame 23 and choose Animation➔Resize Cell (Number of Frames: 5).

17 Click on Frame 23 and choose Effect➡Transition➡Fade. Click OK to use the default settings. This will automatically make the word *magic!* fade into view over five frames. You have finished animating the *magic!* Fade-In layer.

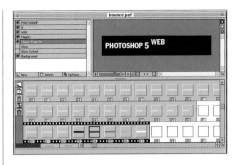

18 Make the Glow layer active and visible. Press the Home key to take you back to Frame 1 on the active (Glow) layer. Choose Animation➡New Cell (Cmd+K) [Ctrl+K]. We don't want to begin seeing the glow until Frame 26, so move this new blank cell to the left of Frame 1 and choose Animation➡Resize Cell (Number of Frames: 26). Click on Frame 27 and choose Animation➡Resize Cell (Number of Frames: 4). You have finished animating the Glow layer.

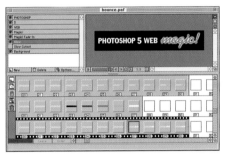

19 Make the Glow Cutout layer active and visible. Press the Home key to take you back to Frame 1 on the active (Glow) layer. Choose Animation➡New Cell (Cmd+K) [Ctrl+K]. We don't want to begin seeing the cutout glow until Frame 28, so move this new blank cell to the left of Frame 1 and choose Animation➡Resize Cell (Number of Frames: 27). Click on Frame 28 and choose Animation➡Resize Cell (Number of Frames: 5). You have finished animating the Glow Cutout layer. Preview the final animation!

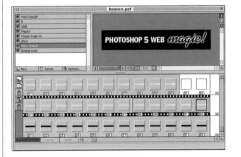

20 Choose Animation➡Frame Rate and set the desired speed of the animation. I chose 4 frames per

51

second. Finally, choose File➦Export and choose the export quality settings you desire for the animated GIF file.

You can view this animation by opening the bounce.htm file located in the Animations folder on the CD-ROM in a Web browser such as Netscape Navigator or Microsoft Internet Explorer. ●

Photo Animator 1.0

This great animation technique makes something look like it is being built brick by brick on screen. In this example, we will animate the Bricks technique found in the Type section, but keep in mind that you could use this animation technique to make just about anything look like it is being constructed on a Web page.

When creating an animation, it is usually a lot easier if you first create the last frame of the animation as a composite image. That way you know what you want to end up with when the animation is complete. To create all of the other animation frames, you can simply duplicate the final composite image multiple times to create as many frames as you will need, modifying each duplicate as necessary.

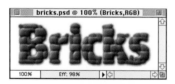

1 Open the bricks.psd file from the Artwork folder on the CD. This file is what you would end up with if you had followed the steps for the Bricks technique starting on page 202. We need to make some adjustments to the layers in this file to facilitate turning it into an animation.

2 Delete the Text and the Mortar layers. Make the Bricks layer active and choose Layer➡Effects➡Create Layer. This will convert the drop shadow from a layer effect into its own layer (Bricks's Drop Shadow).

3 Rename the Background layer 1 Background and move it above the Bricks layer. Duplicate the Bricks layer (Bricks copy), rename it 2, then move it above the 1 Background layer. Hide the Bricks and Bricks's Drop Shadow layers.

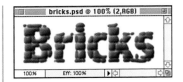

The Background layer should be filled with the color you are using for the background of your Web page and represents the first frame of the animation.

4 Make the 2 layer active if it isn't already. Select the Eraser tool and erase everything in the 2 layer except what you want to see in the second frame of the animation. For this example, I just wanted to see the first row of bricks appear. You just have to decide over how may frames you want the construction to take.

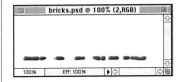

5 Duplicate the Bricks layer (Bricks copy) and rename it 3. Move the 3 layer above the 2 layer. Adjust the opacity of Layer 3 to 30%.

After you move the 3 layer above the 2 layer, you won't be able to see the contents of the 2 layer. You will want to see what the previous frame looks like while you are deciding what the current frame is going to look like. Changing the opacity to 30% allows you to see both frames at once to help you make editing decisions. This technique is called onion skinning.

55

6 Again, with the Eraser tool, erase everything in Layer 3 except what you want to see in the third frame of the animation. Don't worry about erasing anything that has already appeared in the previous frame below. If you leave those pixels visible, it will guarantee that you won't end up with weird blips or gaps in your final animation where you accidentally deleted pixels in one frame but not another.

If you want the building effect to appear a little staggered, skip a few bricks here and there between frames so that certain elements get completed before others in the final animation.

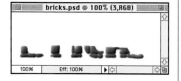

7 When you are finished editing Layer 3, adjust the opacity of the layer to 100%.

8 Repeat steps 5 through 7 for each additional frame of your animation, naming the layers sequentially. For this example, I made 6 more frames to complete the bricks (ending up with layer 9 as the final frame so far.)

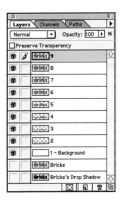

9 For this example I wanted to add two more frames to the animation: one that adds the grout to the bricks, and one that adds a drop shadow for a dramatic final effect.

Duplicate the Bricks layer (Bricks copy) and move it below Layer 9. Switch to default colors and press (Opt+Shift+Delete) [Alt+Shift+Backspace] to fill the Bricks copy layer with the foreground color (black) while preserving transparency.

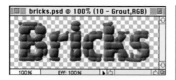

10 Create a new layer and name it 10 - Mortar. Move the 10 - Mortar layer above the 9 layer. Make all layers invisible except 9, 10 - Grout and Bricks copy. Press (Cmd+Opt+Shift+E) [Ctrl+Alt+Shift+E] to create a merged copy of these layers into the 10 - Mortar layer. Delete the Bricks copy layer.

11 Make the Bricks and the Bricks's Drop Shadow layers active. Choose Layer➡Merge Down and rename Bricks's Drop Shadow to 11 Shadow.

12 Move the 11 Shadow layer above the 10 - Mortar layer. Here is what the final Layers palette will look like with all of the layers visible, and the final frame visible in the image window.

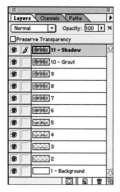

13 Choose File➡Save As and name the file animated bricks.psd. Now all you have to do is bring this entire file into PhotoAnimator, determine the frame rate of the animation, and export it out as an animated GIF.

14 Open PhotoAnimator. (Click the Demo button. The New Animation dialog box will appear. Click the Cancel button.) Choose File➡Open. Locate the animated bricks.psd source file you created in the previous steps and click the Open button.

In the Photoshop Import Options dialog box that appears, choose Horizontal Inline (frames) for the Layer Mapping Options and Bottom to Top for the Layer Import Direction.

15 Choose Animation➡New Layer and name it Background. Move the Background layer below the Layers layer. Because PhotoAnimator preserved the transparency of the imported Photoshop layers, we need to create a separate background layer that repeats the white background across all 11 frames of the animation.

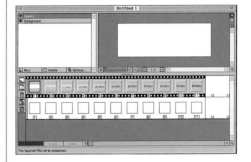

59

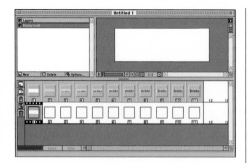

16 You now have two layers: the top layer that contains the 11 frames we created in Photoshop and the bottom layer that is currently blank. We want to duplicate Frame 1 of the top layer (Layers) into Frame 1 of the bottom layer (Background). The quickest way to do this is to simply hold down the (Option) [Alt] key and drag Frame 1 from the Layers layer to Frame 1 of the Background layer.

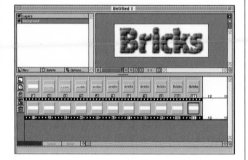

17 Click on Frame 1 in the Background layer. Choose Animation➡Resize Cell (Number of Frames: 11) to extend the white background across the entire animation. (Note: you can also just click on the right border of Frame 1 and drag it just past the Frame 11 marker to do the same thing.)

18 Choose Animation➡Frame Rate. For this example, I chose a frame rate of 1.5 frames per second. You can experiment to determine how fast your image is built. After you set the frame rate, tap the spacebar to preview the animation. If it's too fast or too slow for you, change the frame rate and preview it again until you are happy.

19 Once you are satisfied, choose File➡Export and specify the parameters of your animated GIF file.

20 You can view this animation by opening the bricks.htm file located in the Animations folder on the CD in a Web browser such as Netscape Navigator or Microsoft Internet Explorer. ●

This technique shows how you can use any Photoshop file as a gradient mask to create your own custom transitions. Specifically, you will see how an image created with the Add Noise filter can be used to create a dissolve transition.

For this technique, I have already created the dissolve animation source file and recommend that you use this file to learn how to make the animated effects described in the steps. This animation starts with a solid black background showing, then the word "magic" dissolves into view, so the source file is made with the word "magic" on one layer, and the solid black background on another layer.

1 You will first create a file to use as the gradient mask. Create a file in Photoshop with the same dimensions as the animation (153×53 pixels). Switch to default colors and then fill the Background layer with the foreground color (black) by pressing (Opt+Delete) [Alt+ Backspace]. Choose Filter➡ Noise➡Add Noise (Amount: 200, Gaussian, Monochromatic) and save it as a Photoshop (.psd) file. You will open and use this file later on in the technique.

2 Open PhotoAnimator. (Click the Demo button and the New Animation dialog box will appear. Click the Cancel button.) Choose File➡Open. Open the magic.psd source file from the Artwork on the CD. In the Photoshop Import Options dialog box that appears, choose Vertical Grouped (layers) for the Layer Mapping Options and Top to Bottom for the Layer Import Direction.

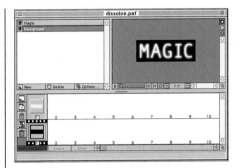

3 Resize the cell on the Magic layer so that it contains 9 frames by clicking on the right cell border and dragging past the Frame 9 indicator. Do the same for the cell on the Background layer.

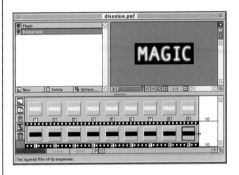

4 Create a new layer (Cmd+L) [Ctrl+L] and name it Dissolve Mask. The new layer should be inserted between the Magic and Background layers. If the layers are not arranged this way at this point, do so now by dragging the layer in the Layer pane to the proper position.

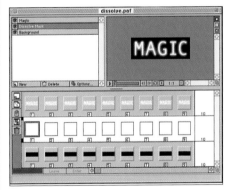

63

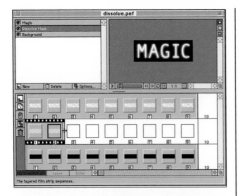

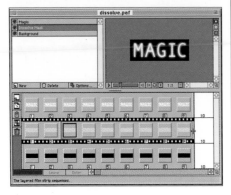

5 Create a new cell on the Dissolve Layer (Cmd+K) [Ctrl+K] and resize it so that it contains 2 frames. We want a slight delay before the word "magic" starts to dissolve into view. This 2-frame cell creates the delay for you. In this example, the word Magic will appear in Frames 1 and 2, then starting in Frame 3, it will disappear and began to dissolve back into view, finishing in Frame 9.

6 We want the dissolve transition to occur over seven frames. Create another new cell on the Dissolve Layer (Cmd+K) [Ctrl+K] and resize it so that it contains 7 frames.

TIP **You can experiment with the timing and delay of this animation. For instance, if you want the viewer to see only a black screen at the start, you could insert a two-frame blank cell at the beginning of the Magic layer, and then resize the second cell to contain only 7 frames, basically repeating the steps you just performed on the Dissolve layer.**

7 Click on Frame 3 in the Dissolve Mask layer and choose Effect➡Transition➡Gradient Mask. Click on the Import button (the open folder icon) and select the dissolve_mask.psd file from the Artwork folder on the CD. For the settings, use Accumulation: Intersection, Direction: White to Black, Mode: None to All, and Edge: 250 levels.

The two settings that have the greatest impact on the transition are the Mode and the Edge. The

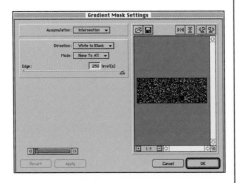

Mode determines how the image being transitioned starts out—either visible and fading away, or hiding and fading into view. The Edge setting determines the intensity of the transition. Experiment with this value to see how it affects the dissolve over time. The Edge value changes the intensity of the transition. You can experiment with this value on your own.

8 That's it! You are pretty much done. If you use the left and right arrow keys on the keyboard you can preview the animation one frame at a time, or tap the spacebar to play the entire animation. As you step from frame to frame, you will see that the first two frames display the word "magic", then starting in frame 3, the word "magic" disappears and begins to dissolve back into view finishing in frame 9.

If you would like to see more examples of different gradient mask transitions, open the crazy_fish.paf file from the Technique Files➡Artwork folder on the CD.

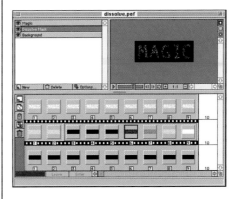

Play the animation. As you can see, this file contains many layers, and most of them are hidden. Leave the Fishy and Background layers visible. All of the other layers are gradient mask transitions. Experiment by turning these layers on and off. Preview the animation to see the results. You can get really crazy if you make more than one gradient mask layer visible.

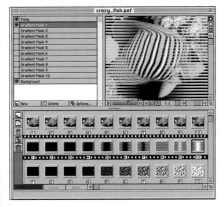

Remember, you can use just about anything as a gradient mask. Simply create a grayscale document in Photoshop and use the Gradient tool or run some filters on it and see what happens! ●

Kite

Sometimes, animations on a Web page can be distracting and annoying to the viewer who is trying to read a lot of text on a page. One way to make animations that are not as obtrusive is to limit the amount of movement in them and build in long delays between animations so that they are not constantly buzzing in the viewer's sight. This technique illustrates that an animation can be interesting and playful, while remaining subtle.

1 Open the kite.psd file from the Artwork folder on the CD-ROM. You will see that the document is made up of two layers (Background and Original Kite).

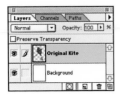

2 We want the first frame in our animation to be a composite of the Background and Original Kite layers. To create this frame, create a new layer and name it Frame 1. With all three layers visible, press (Cmd+Opt+Shift+E) [Ctrl+Alt+Shift+E] to create a merged copy of the Background and Original Kite layers into the Frame 1 layer.

3 For the second frame of the animation, we want the kite to move up, as if it has been caught by a gust of wind. The trick is to get the reference point for the movement to be the end of the string on the left side of the image. Therefore, we can't just move the layer.

Make the Frame 1 layer invisible. Make the Original Kite layer active. Choose Edit➡Free Transform (Cmd+T) [Ctrl+T].

4 You should see a bounding box around the kite with handles in the corners and the sides. By default, the transformation reference point is the center of the bounding box, designated by the cross-hair icon. Photoshop 5 now allows you to relocate the point. Click on the cross-hair icon and drag it to the left edge of the image window where the kite string meets the edge of the window.

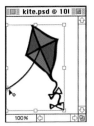

5 Place the cursor outside the bounding box and the cursor icon will now turn into the rotate icon. Rotate the image slightly to the left. You don't need to rotate it very much—remember we want a subtle animation. Press the Enter key to apply the transformation.

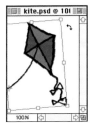

6 Create a new layer and name it Frame 2. There will now be four layers in the file. Move the Frame 2 layer above the Frame 1 layer. Make the Original Kite, Background, and Frame 2 layers visible. Make the Frame 1 layer invisible. Press (Cmd+Opt+Shift+E) [Ctrl+Alt+Shift+E], which combines the rotated kite and the white background to complete Frame 2.

7 Make the Frame 1 and Frame 2 layers invisible. Make the Original Kite layer active. Select the Lasso tool and select the kite's tail. Choose Edit➡Free Transform (Cmd+T) [Ctrl+T]. Move the cross-hair icon from the center of the bounding box to the intersection of the kite tail and the selection. Place the cursor outside the bounding box and the cursor icon will turn into the rotate icon. Rotate the image slightly to the left. Press the Enter key to apply the transformation and then press (Cmd+D)[Ctrl+D] to deselect the kite's tail.

8 Create a new layer and name it Frame 3. Move the Frame 3 layer above the Frame 2 layer. Make the Original Kite, Background, and Frame 3 layers visible and make all the other layers invisible. Press (Cmd+Opt+Shift+E) [Ctrl+Alt+Shift+E] to complete Frame 3.

There you have it. All you need to do now is to export each layer (Frame 1, Frame 2, and Frame 3) to your favorite GIF animation program and set the timing of the movement.

You can view a completed variation of this animation by opening the home.htm file located in the Red Kite Software folder on the CD-ROM in a 4.x or higher version Web browser such as Netscape Navigator 4.x or Microsoft Internet Explorer 4.x. ●

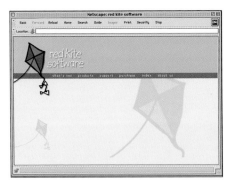

This technique teaches you how to re-create a really cool, multi-glowing text animation, similar to what can be seen at the beginning of the *X-Files* television program.

To pull the animation together, you need to create the individual cells of the animation. Each cell of the animation will be created as a separate Photoshop layer, and the animation will include a total of eight cells. Thus, when you are finished creating the source file, you will have a Photoshop document with eight layers to import into PhotoAnimator.

1 Start by creating the source file for this technique by following the steps or open the multi-glow.psd file located in the Artwork folder on the CD-ROM. Choose File➡Save a Copy to create a backup version of this file.

2 Duplicate the Background layer (Background copy) and rename it Cell 1. Move the Cell 1 layer to the top of the Layers palette and then hide the layer.

3 Make the Text layer active. Switch to default colors. Fill the Text layer with the background color (white) while preserving transparency by pressing (Cmd+Shift+Delete) [Ctrl+Shift+Backspace].

4 Create a new layer (Cell 2). Make the Cell 2, Text, and Background layers visible and hide all the other layers.

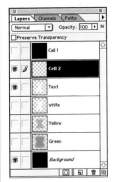

5 Hold down the (Option) [Alt] key and choose Layer➡Merge Visible. This merges copies of the three visible layers as a composite image that will be the second cell of the animation.

6 Hide the Cell 2 and Text layers. Make the White layer active. Create a new layer (Layer 1) and name it Cell 3. Move the Cell 3 layer below the Cell 2 layer. Make sure that the Cell 3, White, and Background layers are visible and make Cell 3 the active layer.

Hold down the (Option) [Alt] key and choose Layer➡Merge Visible.

7 Hide the Cell 3 and White layers. Make the Yellow layer active. Create a new layer (Layer 1) and name it Cell 4. Move the Cell 4 layer below the Cell 3 layer. Make sure that only the Cell 4, Yellow, and Background layers are visible and that the Cell 4 layer is the active layer. Hold down the (Option) [Alt] key and choose Layer➡Merge Visible.

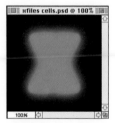

8 Hide the Cell 4 and Yellow layers. Make the Green layer active. Create a new layer (Layer 1) and name it Cell 5. Move the Cell 5 layer below the Cell 4 layer. Make sure that only the Cell 5, Green, and Background layers are visible and that the Cell 5 layer is the active layer. Hold down the (Option) [Alt] key and choose Layer➡Merge Visible.

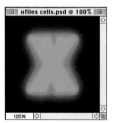

9 Hide the Cell 5 layer. Make the Yellow layer active. Create a new layer (Layer 1) and name it Cell 6. Move the Cell 6 layer below the Cell 5 layer. Make sure that only the Cell 6, Green, Yellow, and Background layers are visible and that the Cell 6 layer is the active layer. Hold down the (Option) [Alt] key and choose Layer➡Merge Visible.

10 Hide the Cell 6 layer. Make the White layer active. Create a new layer (Layer 1) and name it Cell 7. Move the Cell 7 layer below the Cell 6 layer. Make sure that only the Cell 7, Green, Yellow, White, and Background layers are visible and that the Cell 7 layer is the active layer. Hold down the (Option) [Alt] key and choose Layer➡Merge Visible.

11 Hide the Cell 7 layer. Make the Text layer active. Switch to default colors. Fill the Text layer with the foreground color (black) while preserving transparency by pressing (Option+Shift+Delete) [Alt+Shift+Backspace]. Make sure that only the Text, White, Yellow, Green, and Background layers are visible and make the Background layer active. This time DO NOT hold down any key; just choose Layer➡Merge Visible. This merges the original source layers into one layer named Background.

12 Rename the Background layer to Cell 8. You have finished creating the cells of your animation, and you should have eight layers in the document, named Cell 1 through Cell 8. Save and close the Photoshop document.

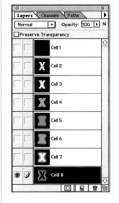

13 Open PhotoAnimator. (Click the Demo button. The New Animation dialog box appears. Click the Cancel button.) Choose File➡ Open. Locate the source file you created in the previous steps and click the Open button.

In the Photoshop Import Options dialog box that appears, choose Horizontal Inline (frames) for the Layer Mapping Options and Top to Bottom for the Layer Import Direction.

This brings the eight Photoshop layers into PhotoAnimator as eight separate cells on one layer.

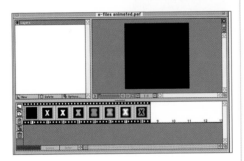

14 PhotoAnimator uses a timeline-based approach to animation. The current animation consists of eight single-frame cells. The default Frame Rate in PhotoAnimator is 10 frames per second. We want the first cell of the animation to show just a solid black image for 0.8 seconds before we see the first solid white X. (Choose Animation➡Frame Rate if you wish to change the default frame rate of the animation.)

To create this frame delay, simply position the cursor over the right-hand border of Frame I and look for it to turn into the double arrow cursor. Once you see the double arrow cursor, drag the border just past Frame 8 and let go.

You have made the first cell now contain eight frames instead of just one. PhotoAnimator automatically repeats the contents across all eight frames.

15 Preview the animation. (You can tap the Spacebar to start and stop the animation preview.) Pretty cool, huh? The only thing left to do is to export the file out as an animated GIF.

16 Choose File➡Export (Format: Animated GIF, Dithering: None, Color Set: Adaptive, Maximum Colors: 128). Make sure the Interframe Transparency Optimization is turned on (checked) and that you set the Loop options to play just one time. Click the Calculate/Preview button to generate a preview and to calculate the file size of the animated GIF using the parameters you chose above.

17 Click the green arrow to play the animation preview. If you are happy with the results, click the Export button. Give the file a name with the three letter extension for GIF files (.GIF) and click the Save button.

If you want to change any parameters of the animated GIF before exporting, such as maximum

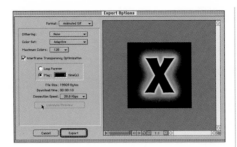

number of colors, change the
settings and then click the
Calculate/ Preview button again
to recalculate based on the new
parameters.

You can view this animation by
opening the multiglow.htm file
located in the Animations folder on
the CD-ROM in a Web browser
such as Netscape Navigator or
Microsoft Internet Explorer. ●

Animated Multiglow

One of the curses of creating cross-platform Web graphics is the limitation of the 216 browser color palette. There are only 216 specific colors that will remain constant and not change on an eight-bit monitor across platforms.

Don't you wish you could use any color you want when creating your GIFs in Photoshop? Maybe at some point a client has given you an illustration that they created in an application other than Photoshop and they didn't have a clue about this Web-safe color issue. Yet, when they hand you the file, they insist that the colors in the file have to be maintained when repurposed for their Web site. This technique will teach you how to create your own custom Web-safe colors. (You might be wondering why this tip is in the Animations section when the technique does not produce an animation. This is a tip that I thought every Web designer would want to know, and should know. This technique describes how to create a custom color for a standard (single image) GIF. You can apply the same technique in your GIF animations because a GIF animation is simply made up of multiple GIFs.)

1 Open the tatoo.psd file from the Artwork folder on the CD. At first glance, this graphic looks normal. It is an RGB file and all the solid colors look great.

2 If you change your monitor's color display setting to 8-bit (256 colors), you will see that those nice solid colors aren't nice and solid anymore. The colors in the original image were not in the 216 color palette that we had to choose from.

 While using Photoshop 5.0, if you want to see the Web safe colors display correctly when your monitor is set to display only 256 colors, you must choose File➔Preferences➔Color Settings➔RGB Setup and turn off the Display Using Monitor Compensation checkbox.

3 The magic behind creating your own custom Web-safe colors is to create a hybrid color. A hybrid color is formed by combining four pixels of two different colors from the 216-color Web-safe palette together in a 2x2 pixel pattern that will look like a new composite color when viewed on-screen. Let's begin by dealing with the red hearts.

First, we should sample the color we are trying to match. Select the Eyedropper tool and click any-where in the red heart color. Open the Color palette and you will see that this color is RGB: 176, 30, 36. Create a new document (2×2 pix-els, Contents: White). Zoom up to 1600%.

4 Choose Window➔Show Swatches. If you do not have the 216-color Web-safe palette loaded into the Swatches palette already,

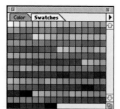

choose Replace Swatches from the Swatches palette menu by clicking on the black triangle in the upper right corner of the palette. In the Open dialog box that appears, click the Find button and enter Web Safe Colors into the Find field without the quotes. Photoshop will find the file for you; open it once it does. The Swatches Palette will now display the 216 web-safe colors.

5 The trick now is to find the two closest colors in the palette to the color you sampled from the heart, and set them as your foreground and background colors. Since this is a book and I can't point to your screen and show you where the two colors are in the Swatches palette, I'll cheat and give you the RGB values. The foreground color is 153, 0, 0 and the background color is 204, 51, 51. Select the Pencil tool and choose the smallest brush size from the Brushes palette.

You will have to experiment with finding colors in the palette to match a color in an image. Generally, the best way to do this is through trial and error until you get the hang of it. Pretend that the color you are trying to match is the middle color between the two you need to choose from the 216 Web-safe colors.

Paint the upper left corner and the lower right corner with the foreground color. Press the X key to exchange the foreground color with the background color. Paint the lower left corner and the upper right corner with the other color.

SAFE COLORS

6 Select All, then choose
Edit→Define Pattern. Make the
tattoo.psd file active again. Select
the Magic Wand tool. Press the
Enter key to open the Magic Wand
Options palette. Turn off the Anti-
aliased checkbox. Click in the red
heart area and choose
Select→Similar to select all of the
red color in the image.

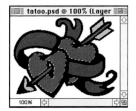

7 Choose Edit→Fill (Contents Use:
Pattern, Opacity: 100%, Mode:
Normal, Preserve Transparency
turned off). Deselect the selection.

Now you have a custom color that
matches the original (or pretty
dang close), and won't change
regardless of the viewer's monitor
setting. You can repeat this process
for every color you wish to match
in the original illustration.

TIP Is there an easier way to
accomplish this? Yes! With
ColorSafe from Boxtop
Software. You will find a
fully functional shareware
version of this wonderful
plug-in in the Software
folder on the CD. If you
end up adding it to your
collection of tools, remember to support shareware
developers by paying the
shareware fee. ●

This technique shows you how to create a banner ad animation that looks like a spotlight is moving over a black background, revealing words as it passes over them. You will use a unique feature in PhotoAnimator that allows you to animate a mask between two content layers.

Creating the Animation Source Files

1 Create a new document the size of a typical banner ad (468 × 60, white).

2 Choose the Type tool and create the text for the banner ad. For flexibility, I created each item on its own layer.

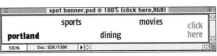

3 I wanted to emphasize the words "click here," so in addition to coloring them red (RGB: 255, 0, 0), I quickly added a drop shadow to the layer using the new layer effects in Photoshop 5. Choose Layer➡Effects➡Drop Shadow (Mode: Normal, Opacity: 40%, Angle: 135, Distance: 1, Blur: 0, Intensity: 0%).

click
here

TOOLBOX

PhotoAnimator 1.0

After you apply the Drop Shadow layer effect, you will notice a layer effects icon to the right of the layer name. If you want to edit the layer effect, simply double-click this icon to open a particular layer effect dialog box.

4 Choose Layer➡Flatten Image. Change the name of the Background layer to Banner Text. Create a new layer and name it Black. Switch to default colors. Fill the Black layer with the foreground color (black) by pressing (Option+Delete) [Alt+Backspace]. Choose File➡Save. Name the document spot banner.psd and save it as a .psd file.

5 We'll create the spotlight mask in a separate file. Create a new document (120 × 120, white). Turn on the rulers and create vertical and horizontal guides that intersect at 60 and 60. These guides help you create your elements from the center of the document.

6 Choose the Elliptical Marquee tool. Press the Enter key to open the Marquee Options palette. Choose Fixed Size from the Style pop-up menu and enter 100 into the Width and Height fields. Position the cursor at the intersection of the ruler guides. Hold down the (Option) [Alt] key and click to create a perfect 100 × 100 pixel circle selection from the center of the document.

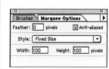

83

7 Switch to default colors. Fill the selection with the foreground color (black) by pressing Option+Delete) [Alt+Backspace]. Deselect the selection and choose File➡Save. Name the document spotmask.psd and save it as a Photoshop file.

Creating the Animation

8 Open PhotoAnimator. Choose File➡Open and locate the spot banner.psd file you saved in Step 4. In the Photoshop Import Options dialog box that appears, choose Vertical Grouped (layers) for the Layer Mapping Options and Top to Bottom for the Layer Import Direction. Make sure that only Layer Images is checked for the Import Items and click the Import button.

9 Click Frame 1 of the Black layer. Choose Animation➡Resize Cell (32 frames). Repeat this step for Frame 1 of the Banner Text layer.

10 Choose Animation➡New Layer (Cmd+L) [Ctrl+L] and name it Spot Mask. You should now have three layers listed in the Layers Pane in the upper-left corner of the window. The Spot Mask layer should be the middle layer. For the rest of the steps, only modify the Spot Mask layer. The Black and Banner Text layers are finished already.

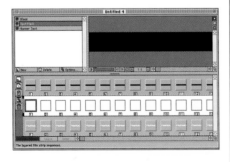

11 Choose Animation➡New Cell (Cmd+K) [Ctrl+K]. Repeat this step again to create a second cell on the Spot Mask layer. Click Frame 2 of the Spot Mask layer and choose Animation➡Resize Cell (five frames). The Spot Mask layer now contains two cells—a one-frame cell (Frame 1) and a five-frame cell (Frames 2 through 6). The gray vertical bar separates the two cells.

12 Select Frame 2 of the Spot Mask layer. Choose Effect➡Mask➡ Repeat. Click the file folder icon and locate the spotmask.psd file you saved in Step 7. Use the settings shown: Default Fill: White, Accumulation: Intersection. Click the bottom-left corner of the left Location grid. Change the X value to 10 and the Y value to 10. Turn on the Move To checkbox. Click the bottom-left corner of the right Location grid. Change the X value to 150 and the Y value to -70. Click OK.

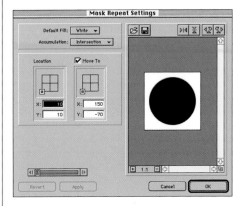

You can preview the animation frame by frame by using the left and right arrow keys on the keyboard.

Start on Frame 1 and use the right arrow key to see Frames 1 through 6. You will see a "spotlight" appear, revealing the word "Portland." The spotlight stops in Frame 6. All you have left to do is create several duplicates of this second cell, and change the start and end positions of the mask.

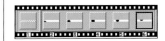

85

13 Select Frame 2 of the Spot Mask layer; then copy and paste. This places a duplicate of the second cell to the right of the second cell. Double-click Frame 7. In the left set of Location controls (the Start position), set the X value to 120 and the Y value to 0. In the right set of Location controls (the End position), set the X value to 200 and the Y value to 70.

14 Select Frame 7 of the Spot Mask layer. Copy and paste. Double-click Frame 12. Change the Start position X value to 220 and the Y value to 50. Change the End position X value to 280 and the Y value to −20.

15 Select Frame 12 of the Spot Mask layer. Copy and paste. Double-click Frame 17. Change the Start position X value to 300 and the Y value to 0. Change the End position X value to 390 and the Y value to 50.

16 Select Frame 17 of the Spot Mask layer. Copy and paste. Double-click Frame 22. Turn off the Move To check box. Change the Location X value to 390 and the Y value to 50.

You're done!

Turn on the Loop option by clicking the Loop button, underneath the preview window.

Press the Spacebar to preview the animation. All that's left to do is to choose File➡Export and set the parameters of the animated GIF file.

You can view this animation by opening the spotbanner.htm file located in the Animations folder on the CD-ROM in a Web browser, such as Netscape Navigator or Microsoft Internet Explorer. ●

Transitions can turn a boring animation into one that really gets noticed and makes people ask, How did they do that? This technique shows you how easy it can be to add interesting transitions to your animations.

For this technique, I have already created the wipe animation source file, and I suggest that you use this file to learn how to make the animated effects described in the steps. For this example, I want the animation to start with a solid black background, then the word HOCUS will wipe into view from left to right. Finally, the word HOCUS will turn into POCUS in a top to bottom wipe.

The source file has a Background layer and separate layers for the word HOCUS and the letter P. In addition, there are two blank layers named Top to Bottom and Right to Left. These will be the layers we create the wipe transitions in.

1 Open PhotoAnimator. (Click the Demo button. The New Animation dialog box will appear. Click the Cancel button.)

2 Choose File➡Open. Open the wipe.psd source file from the Artwork folder on the CD.

In the Photoshop Import Options dialog box that appears, choose Vertical Grouped (layers) for the Layer Mapping Options and Top to Bottom for the Layer Import Direction.

TOOLBOX

PhotoAnimator
1.0

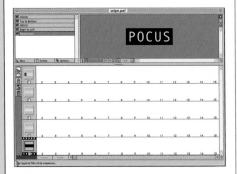

3 Resize the cell on the Background layer so that it contains 14 frames by clicking on the right cell border and dragging past the Frame 14 indicator.

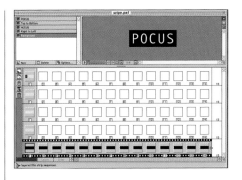

4 Resize the cell on the Right to Left layer so that it contains 2 frames. Create a new cell on the Right to Left layer (Cmd+K) [Ctrl+K] and resize it so that it contains 6 frames.

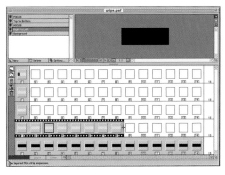

5 Choose Effect➥Transition➥Wipe and use the default settings. PhotoAnimator automatically creates the wipe frames for you, in this case, over 6 frames, with each frame revealing a bit more of the image as the animation moves from right to left.

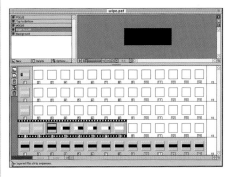

6 We want the animation to start out showing a solid black background for the first two frames. To accomplish this, insert a blank cell in front of Frame 1 on the HOCUS layer. Click on the *left* cell border of the cell on the HOCUS layer, drag just pass the Frame 2 indicator, and let go. This automatically inserts a blank, two-frame cell in front of the existing cell on that layer.

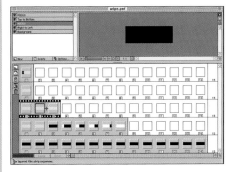

89

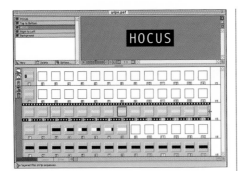

7 Resize the second cell on the HOCUS layer so that it contains 12 frames by clicking on the right cell border and dragging it past the Frame 14 indicator.

You've just created your wipe effect! Click on Frame 3 on the HOCUS layer. Look in the Preview pane and you will see a black background. Click on Frame 4 and you will see the letter H revealed, on Frame 5 the letter O will be revealed, and so on until Frame 8, where the word is completely revealed.

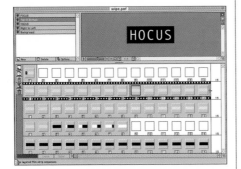

8 Resize the cell on the Top to Bottom layer so that it contains 8 frames. Create a new cell on the Top to Bottom layer (Cmd+K) [Ctrl+K] and resize it so that it contains 6 frames.

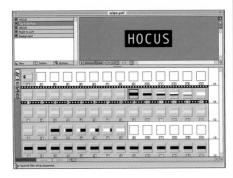

9 Choose Effect➡Transition➡Wipe. Change the Direction to Top to Bottom. PhotoAnimator automatically creates the wipe frames for you, in this case, over 6 frames, with each frame revealing a little bit more of the image as the transition moves from top to bottom.

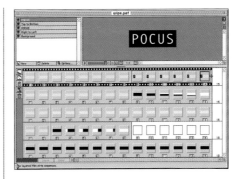

10 We don't want the word HOCUS to start changing into POCUS until Frame 9. To accomplish this, insert a blank cell in front of Frame 1 on the POCUS layer. As you did on the HOCUS layer, click on the LEFT cell border of the cell on the POCUS layer, drag it past the Frame 8 indicator and let go. This automatically inserts a blank eight-frame cell in front of the existing cell on that layer.

Resize the second cell on the POCUS layer so that it contains 6 frames by clicking on the right cell border and dragging it to just past the Frame 14 indicator. That's it, you're done! Tap the spacebar to play the preview.

 Don't forget about all the other transitions available. Experiment with the Barn Door and Fade transitions available from the Effect➥Transition menu. As a rule, Wipe and Barn Door transitions result in much smaller file sizes for the exported animated GIF than Fade and Gradient Mask transitions.

I have combined the above technique with the Dissolve technique on page 62 to create a much more complex animation. You can view this animation by opening the hocus_pocus.htm file located in the Animations folder on the CD-ROM in a Web browser such as Netscape Navigator or Microsoft Internet Explorer. ●

WIPE WIP

PART II

Buttons

Nothing illustrates the interface experience of a Web page better than an effectively designed button or navigation bar. This section provides many techniques for creating a variety of buttons and is meant to encourage you to go behind just the basic beveled buttons. Sometimes, something as simple as word on a solid color bar that changes color as the mouse goes over it can be more effective than a wild 3D looking button.

Some of the buttons created here are interactive, meaning they use a JavaScript code that swaps out one graphic for another when the user passes their mouse over it. In those situations, you will need to create two "states" for the rollover button effect to be complete. You will find the JavaScript code described in the Nav Bar technique, and you can see actual examples by opening the respective HTML documents in a Web Browser. All files and their locations are referenced at the end of each technique.

PhotoButton

How do you make buttons for your Web page that go beyond the basic bevel? Use a plug-in that was designed just to create buttons called PhotoButton, a component of the PhotoTools collection of Photoshop plug-ins. If you do not have Extensis PhotoTools, you can find a 30-day fully functional demo version in the Software folder on the CD-ROM.

1 Create a new document. My example is 300×200 pixels. Rename the Background layer Buttons. Choose Filter→PhotoTools→ PhotoButton 2.0. Click the Reset button to make sure you start at the same spot as this technique.

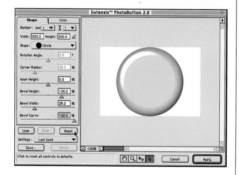

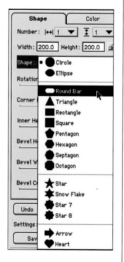

2 The first thing you should do is decide what shape you want your button or buttons to be. Click on the Shape pop-up menu in the Shape tab. You have 16 different shapes to choose from. I chose Round Bar.

3 PhotoButton automatically makes the button you choose proportionally as large as the canvas allows. If you know that you want your buttons to have specific pixel dimensions, turn on the Lock button to the right of the Height field and enter those values in the Width and Height fields. I used Width: 250, Height: 50.

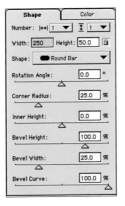

4 The rest of the controls in the Shape tab are fun to experiment with and allow you to customize the button shape and bevel. If you enter a negative value for the Inner Height, you will create an "innie-button," and if you use a positive number, you will create an "outie-button." I used Rotation Angle: 0, Corner Radius: 100%, Inner Height: 100%, Bevel Height: 50%, Bevel Width: 25%, and Bevel Curve: 50%.

5 One of the nice things about PhotoButton is that it can create multiple buttons at the same time. Once you have decided how the buttons should look, decide how many buttons you want to make. I chose to make 3 buttons, arranged vertically.

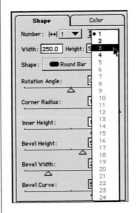

PhotoButton

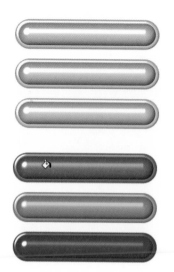

6 Click on the Color tab. Select the Paint Bucket tool and choose a color from the Paint Color pop-up menu. You can use the Paint Bucket tool to color every part of each button individually. You can color the background (Outer), the beveled edge (Bevel), and the inner surface (Inner)—just click on the portion you want to paint with the Paint Bucket tool. If you want all the inner parts or beveled edges to be the same color, you can hold down the (Opt) [Alt] key when you click on one of those parts to color them all at the same time.

7 You can also control the surface qualities of the button—how shiny or matte the buttons will be. In the Color tab, click on the Inner tab and choose a surface quality from the Preset menu. I chose Rubber. You can also set the surface quality for the beveled edge by clicking on the Bevel tab and choosing a sur-face quality from the Preset menu. Again, I chose Rubber.

8 Lastly, you may want these buttons to end up on a transparent background for use on your Web page. To do so, in the Color tab, click on the Outer tab and turn on the Transparent check box. Click the Apply button.

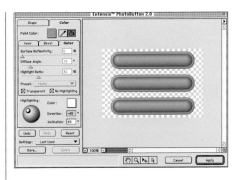

VARIATIONS

Here are some examples of the different types of buttons you can create quickly with PhotoButton. Just choose a different shape and play with the bevel, color, and surface controls.

You can even create your buttons out of a texture. Open PhotoButton on a layer that contains the texture you want on your buttons and choose the color None from the Paint Color pop-up menu in the Color tab before using the Paint Bucket tool. In this example, I used the Acid Rain texture created in the technique found on page 162.

TOOLBOX

PhotoBevel Solo

There are a zillion and one ways to create 3D beveled buttons for your Web page, from quick and easy to hard and complex. Although there is something to be said for hand-rolling your beveled effects, sometimes it's a lot smarter to cut a few corners and let a plug-in do most of the work for you. This technique highlights such a plug-in, Extensis PhotoBevel. This filter is available to you in the Software folder on the CD-ROM and is yours to keep for FREE. It is not a shareware or time-limited plug-in.

1 Create a new document. My example is 125×195 pixels. Choose a foreground color that matches the color you will use for the background of your Web page. I chose RGB: 254, 254, 173. Fill the Background layer with this foreground color by pressing (Opt+Delete) [Alt+Backspace].

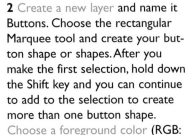

2 Create a new layer and name it Buttons. Choose the rectangular Marquee tool and create your button shape or shapes. After you make the first selection, hold down the Shift key and you can continue to add to the selection to create more than one button shape. Choose a foreground color (RGB: 62, 121, 168) and fill the selection(s) with the foreground color by pressing (Opt+Delete) [Alt+Backspace]. Deselect the selection.

3 Choose Filter➡Extensis➡ PhotoBevel Solo. You can control the bevel's type, shape, width, edge softness, the highlight and shadow colors, intensity and balance, as well as the direction of the light source. You can also save your settings to re-create your bevel effects instantly for a future project. PhotoBevel also has multiple undo/redo (Cmd+Z/Cmd+Y) [Ctrl+Z/Ctrl+Y], so feel free to experiment with the settings.

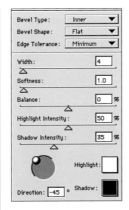

I used Bevel Type: Inner, Bevel Shape: Flat, Edge Tolerance: Minimum, Width: 4, Softness: 1.0, Balance: 0%, Highlight Intensity: 50%, Shadow Intensity: 35%.

VARIATIONS

The following variations were all created in similar ways and are presented here to illustrate the variety of bevel shapes and effects available in PhotoBevel. Each document was made up of two layers: a Background layer that matched the background color of the Web page, and a type layer on which the beveled objects were created.

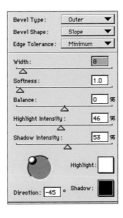

To make this text look like it has been punched from behind the background, I used an Outer Slope setting.

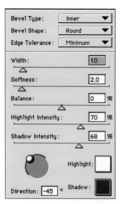

Here, I used an Inner Round setting. You can change the effect dramatically by experimenting with the Highlight and Shadow colors, as well as their Intensity settings. If you click on a color pop-up chart, you will see a real-time preview of the colors you choose as you move the mouse across different swatches.

For this industrial strength type, I used an Inner Slope setting.

To create this old-style cast-metal bevel, I used an Inner Flat setting with an extreme Width setting.

You can view these examples as GIF animations by opening the bevels.htm file located in the Animations folder on the CD-ROM in a Web browser such as Netscape Navigator or Microsoft Internet Explorer. ●

103

curled page button

Hot off the press! Here is an interesting technique to create buttons for your Web page that look like curled pages. You will use the Shear filter on a basic rectangular shape to add this dimensional perspective.

1 Create a new document (200 × 200, white).

2 Create a new layer (Layer 1). Select the Rectangular Marquee tool and make a rectangular selection in the center of the image. You can create the shape and size of your page with this selection. Make sure there is enough room around the selection to allow for curling and rotation later. My selection is 100 × 150 pixels.

3 Choose a foreground color for the color of the curled page (RGB: 255, 255, 204). Fill the selection with the foreground color by pressing (Option+Delete) [Alt+Backspace]. Deselect the selection.

4 Choose a foreground color for the text on the curled page. Then select the Type tool and create the text. The text you create will end up on its own layer above Layer 1.

5 More than likely, you will want to align the centers of these two layers (the text layer and Layer 1). Photoshop 5 has a great new alignment feature! Link the text layer with Layer 1 and make sure Layer 1 is the selected layer.

Choose Layer➡Align Linked➡ Vertical Center. Choose Layer➡ Align Linked➡Horizontal Center. The text is now perfectly centered over the page shape on Layer 1. Choose Layer➡Merge Linked to combine the text layer and Layer 1 into one layer.

6 To curl the page, choose Filter➡Distort➡Shear and create a slender S shape on the grid as shown here.

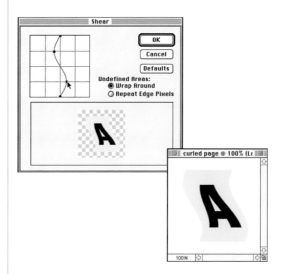

7 To change the angle of the page so that it looks to be floating in space, choose Edit➡Transform➡ Numeric and enter 70 degrees for the Rotate Angle. How you want your page oriented is up to you. The further away you move from the horizontal axis, the harder it will be to read whatever text you place on the curled page.

curled
page
button

8 To add some depth and realism to this page, you will want to add some shading. Create a new layer (Layer 2) and set its Blend mode to Multiply. (Cmd-click) [Ctrl-click] Layer 1 in the Layers palette to create a selection on Layer 2 in the shape of the curled page. This keeps you from painting outside the lines as you paint in the shading details. Working in Layer 2 protects Layer 1 as you add the shading. The shading details you add to the page are up to you, and you will want to be able to make adjustments as you go without having to start all over.

9 Choose a foreground color for the shading (RGB: 153, 153, 0). Choose the Brush or Airbrush tool and an appropriate brush size (try a 35-pixel, soft-edged brush). You can type any number on the keyboard to set the opacity of the brush. Start with a low opacity, such as 10%, by typing the 1 key. Paint in the shading detail on the page you want. When you are happy with the results, deselect the selection. Choose Layer➡Merge Down.

10 Duplicate Layer 1 (Layer 1 copy) and rename it Shadow. Move the Shadow layer below Layer 1. Switch to default colors. Fill the Shadow layer with the foreground color (black) while preserving transparency by pressing (Option+Shift+Delete) [Alt+Shift+Backspace]. This adds a cast shadow behind the page.

11 Choose Edit➡Free Transform (Cmd+T) [Ctrl+T]; then rotate, skew, and position the shadow where you want it. Press the Enter key to apply the transformation to the Shadow layer.

12 Set the Opacity of the Shadow layer to 20%. Choose Filter➡Blur➡ Gaussian Blur (Radius: 4) to make the edges a little more fuzzy.

These pages make a nice collection of buttons on a navigation bar.

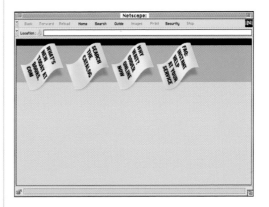

108

Just about every Web page you see these days has buttons and things to click on. Here is one of the easiest button-making techniques that enables you to work with the flexibility of layers.

This particular technique is ideal for round and elliptical buttons.

1 Create a new document (200 × 200, Transparent). Turn on the rulers and create vertical and horizontal guides that intersect at 100 and 100. These guides help you create your elements from the center of the document.

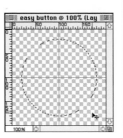

2 Select the Elliptical Marquee tool. Align the cursor with the intersection of the guides and drag out a shape for your button. Press the (Option) [Alt] key to create your selection from the center. Hold down the Shift key if you want to create a perfect circle.

3 Choose a foreground color. Fill the selection by pressing (Option+Delete) [Alt+Backspace]. Deselect the selection. Turn off the rulers and make the guides invisible. Duplicate Layer 1 (Layer 1 copy).

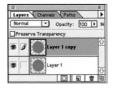

4 Switch to default colors. Fill **Layer 1** with the foreground color while preserving transparency by pressing (Option+Shift+Delete) [Alt+Shift+Backspace].

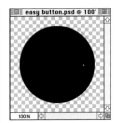

5 Choose Filter➡Blur➡Gaussian Blur. Set the Radius proportional to how raised you want your button to be: the higher the radius, the more depth your button will have. I used 6 pixels.

6 Choose Filter➡Stylize➡Emboss. Angle determines the direction of the light source. For some reason, I always use 135; it just feels right. For Height, use the same amount you used for your Gaussian Blur Radius in Step 5.

7 Set the layer's blending mode to Hard Light. After you run the Emboss filter, you end up with a gray layer on top of your original shape layer. Choosing Hard Light ignores the "soft light" (midtones) of the gray layer and only applies the "hard light" (highlights and shadows) to the underlying layer.

8 Finally, group Layer 1 copy with Layer 1 by pressing (Cmd+G) [Ctrl+G]. This trims the edges of the button, removing the haze left over from when you blurred the layer in Step 5.

VARIATIONS

Other Shapes

Instead of creating a circle, I used the Polygon Lasso tool to create this starburst in Step 2.

Textures

Here I filled the button with the Acid Rain texture shown on page 162 by creating the texture on a layer above the button shape layer (Layer 1) and then choosing Layer→Group with Previous.

Multicolored Buttons

To create this variation, create a new layer above Layer 1. Make a rectangular selection that overlaps half of the original button shape and fill it with a color. Then choose Layer➥Group with Previous. ●

Here's a technique that produces very realistic 3D buttons. The cool part about this effect is that you can make the surface of the button raised or in relief. (Or in lay terms, you can make the button an "innie" or an "outie.") You will use three additional channels to create these buttons.

1 Your button should be a white shape on a black background. The object you engrave should be black. If you want to use my artwork, you can find gear.psd on the CD-ROM in Technique Files➡Artwork.

TIP **Creating complex shapes in Photoshop alone can be a challenge at times. Depending on your experience with other applications, you might be more comfortable creating the building blocks in an illustration application such as Adobe Illustrator or Macromedia FreeHand. If you choose to go this route, save the vector illustration file as an EPS file and Photoshop converts it to pixels for you when you open it in Photoshop.**

2 Duplicate the Blue channel three times. Change the name of the Alpha 1 channel to Outside. Change the name of the Alpha 2 channel to Inside. Change the name of the Alpha 3 channel to Lighting FX.

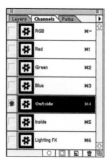

3 Make the Outside channel active. Choose the Lasso tool and draw a selection around the inside shape of the button. Fill the selection with the foreground color (white) by pressing (Option+Delete) [Alt+Backspace]. Deselect the selection. This creates the mask you will use to isolate the button shape.

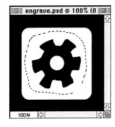 

4 Make the Inside channel active. Select the Magic Wand tool and click on the black object on the button. Inverse the selection.

5 Fill the selection with the background color (black) by pressing (Cmd+Delete) [Ctrl+Backspace]. Inverse the selection again and fill it with the foreground color (white) by pressing (Option+Delete) [Alt+Backspace]. Deselect the selection. This creates the mask you use to isolate the shape on the button.

6 Make the Lighting FX channel active. (Cmd+click) [Ctrl+click] on the Outside channel to load it as a selection. Choose Select➥Modify➥Contract. The number you enter here determines how high the bevel of the button will be. I chose 5 pixels.

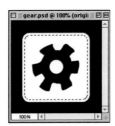

7 Inverse the selection and choose Filter➥Blur➥Gaussian Blur (Radius: 5). Inverse the selection again and choose Filter➥Blur➥Gaussian Blur again (Radius: 1.5). Deselect the selection. Blurring the button shape and the object on the button slightly makes the 3D illusion more realistic.

113

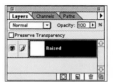

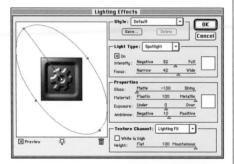

8 Whew! The hard part is over. Now you get to make the creative decisions. Return to the composite channel. Switch to default colors. Fill the layer named Original with the background color (white) by pressing (Cmd+Delete) [Ctrl+Backspace]. Rename the Original layer to Raised. (Note: if you use your own artwork instead of the gear.psd file, you can create a new layer, name it Original, and fill with white; then do Step 8.)

9 Choose Filter➡Render➡Lighting Effects (Texture Channel: Lighting FX, White is high off). Use the settings shown here or choose the Raised button preset from the pop-up menu.

TIP If you want to use the same settings again for another button, you can click the Save button and give the Style a name.

10 Press (Cmd+Option+4) [Ctrl+Alt+4] to load the Outside channel as a selection. Inverse the selection and press the Delete key. Deselect the selection. This cuts the button out of the background.

11 Create a new layer and name it Button Object. Press (Cmd+Option+5) [Ctrl+Alt+5] to load the Inside channel as a selection. Choose a light gray for the foreground color (RGB: 165, 165, 165) and fill the selection by pressing (Option+Delete) [Alt+Backspace]. Deselect the selection.

VARIATIONS

Relief Buttons
For this relief variation, I turned on the White Is High check box in Step 7. (Or choose the Relief button preset from the pop-up menu.)

Buttons for Rollovers
A popular effect on the Web is a button rollover where the button changes as the mouse moves over it. To achieve this, you need two different graphics: one that represents the "off" state and one that represents the "on" state. A simple variation is to choose a different foreground color other than the gray (RGB: 255, 255, 153) in Step 9 and fill the Background Object layer with it while preserving transparency (Option+Shift+Delete) [Alt+Shift+Backspace].

115

Colorizing

To colorize the entire button instead of just the object on the button, I created a new adjustment layer above the Button Object layer by choosing Layer➡New➡ Adjustment Layer and selecting Hue/Saturation from the Type pop-up menu. After clicking OK, turn on the Colorize check box in the Hue/Saturation dialog box and choose the Hue, Saturation, and Lightness values that suit you.

To control the colors of the button and the object on the button separately, move the Hue/Saturation Adjustment layer below the Button Object layer. ●

By now, anyone who has surfed the Web has seen interactive rollovers where a graphic will change appearance when the mouse rolls over it. In this technique, you will see how to use a JavaScript rollover to create an effective navigation bar. Once the user moves to another page from the home page, the navigation bar should display the path the user took to get to the current page. Then, at any time, if the user wants to navigate back to a previous page, they have the ability to quickly jump back to any section along the current path without having to click the browser's Back button multiple times.

You will need to make two graphics for every button you want to display—one each for the on and off states of the buttons.

1 Create a new document. My example is 600×17 pixels. Choose a foreground color for the navigation bar in its off-state. I chose RGB: 102, 102, 0. Fill the Background layer with this foreground color by pressing (Option+Delete) [Alt+Backspace]. Rename the Background layer Nav Bar.

2 Create a new layer and name it Rollover. Choose a foreground color (RGB: 62, 121, 168) and fill the Rollover layer with the foreground color by pressing (Opt+Delete) [Alt+Backspace]. The Rollover layer will contain the buttons in their On state. Because the focus of this button bar is on navigation, I decided to create a subtle effect. A simple change of color for the buttons as the mouse passes

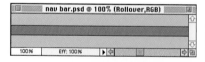

over them is all that is needed here. Of course, you can make the on buttons look any way you want. Some other options are to make the text glow, or have a drop shadow appear.

3 Create the text for the buttons you are working on. The type will end up on its own layer. Rename the text layer Nav Bar Text. I chose white for my text color.

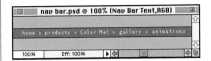

The most efficient way to create this navigation bar in Photoshop is to type out the entire path to the last page in the section you are working on for your web site. For this example, the Web site is for a software company that makes software for children. On the home page, the main level links are What's New, Products, Support, Purchase, Index, and About Us.

We will be working on the Products path. In this example I have typed out the path that takes me to a page that displays sample animations. The path is home➡products➡Color Me!➡gallery➡animations.

By creating the entire path at once, we can simply slice and dice the Photoshop file into the separate pieces we will need for each on and off button.

4 Show the rulers (Cmd+R) [Ctrl+R] and add vertical guides that indicate the width of each button. You will use these guides to quickly select each button shape. After you have created the guides, make sure the Snap to Guides option is turned on by choosing View➡Snap to Guides.

5 Make the Rollover layer invisible. With the Rectangular Marquee tool, select the first button shape, dragging it from guide to guide.

6 Choose Edit→Copy Merged (Cmd+Shift+C) [Ctrl+ Shift+C]. This will copy the contents of all the visible layers within the selection to the clipboard. The regular Copy command would only copy the contents of the active layer within the selection to the clipboard.

Create a new document and accept the settings that are in the New dialog box. (Photoshop automatically enters the properties of whatever is on the clipboard into the New dialog box.) Paste the contents of the clipboard into the new document.

TIP When creating the new document, jot down the width and height values for future reference. If you are creating the HTML code manually, you will need to know the width and height of your graphics.

7 Choose File→Export→Gif89a Export. Select the attributes that you would like the resulting GIF file to have. When it comes time to name the file, add OFF to the end of the name. For this example, I created the off button for home, so I would name the button homeOFF.gif. After you are finished with the export, close the Untitled-1 file without saving changes.

8 Now, we will make the on button. Make the Rollover layer visible. Choose Edit➡Copy Merged (Cmd+Shift+C) [Ctrl+ Shift+C].

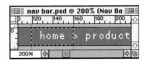

9 Create a new document and accept the settings that are in the New dialog box. Choose Edit➡Paste (Cmd+V) [Ctrl+V].

10 Choose File➡Export➡Gif89a Export. Select the attributes that you would like the resulting GIF file to have. When it comes time to name the file, add ON to the end of the name. For this example, I created the on button for home, so I would name the button homeON.gif.

11 Repeat Steps 5 through 9 for each additional on and off button you need to make.

The JavaScript Code

If you are creating your web pages by manually typing in the HTML and JavaScript code, then you will need to know the magic behind the rollover effect. Don't be scared! It's easy! Here's the code:

```
<A HREF="home.htm"
onMouseOver="document.home.s
rc='homeON.gif'"
onMouseOut="document.home.sr
c='homeOFF.gif'"➡
<img src="homeOFF.gif"
width=41 height=17
name="home"➡
</A>
```

Now, what the heck does all of that mean?

A HREF='home.htm' — this is where you type in the URL of the page you want the user to go to when they actually click on the button.

The easiest way to work with images in JavaScript is to name them. Names must be one word, contain no spaces, and they can't begin with a number—other than that, you can name things anything you want.

In this example, name='home' defines the image being linked as a graphic named home. This part, img src='homeOFF.gif', is the actual link to the image that is viewed when the page loads.

This part, onMouseOver='docu-ment.home.src='homeON.gifí', can be translated to mean: In the docu-ment, there is an item named home when a mouse moves over it, that item should be represented by the graphic homeON.gif. Of course, onMouseOut='document.home.src=' homeOFF.gifí' means that item should be changed to homeOFF.gif when the mouse moves off it. It's simple.

You can copy and paste this code wherever you want a new rollover effect to occur, and all you have to do is change the word home to the name of the new graphic wherever it occurs in the code.

The last graphic in the bar will not be a button so it won't need the JavaScript code. You don't need the button to do anything because it represents the page the user is actually on at the time.

I have created a page with this navigation bar in it along with other elements for a mock children's software company. You can view this example and see the navigation bar in action by opening the home.htm file located in the ➥Red Kite Software folder on the CD in a Web browser such as Netscape Navigator 4.0 or higher, or Microsoft Internet Explorer 4.0 and higher (You may see unexpected results if you view these pages in an earlier version). Once opened, click on the products button. This takes you to the products page, and the navigation bar changes to show just the current path (home➥products). View the source code to see the JavaScript I used. ●

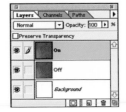

TOOLBOX

PhotoTools 2.0

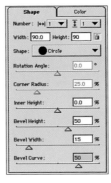

This technique will show you how to make a button that appears to be pushed outward towards the viewer as they move their mouse over it. To pull this off, you will need to create two graphics—the on and off states of the button—and a JavaScript.

1 Create a new document. My example is 100×100 pixels. Create a new layer and name it Off. Fill the Off layer with a texture of your choice (see any of the texture techniques on pages XX through XX for ideas). After you have created your texture, duplicate the Off layer (Off copy) and rename the layer On.

2 Make the On layer invisible and make the Off layer active. Choose Filter➡PhotoTools➡PhotoButton 2.0. (If this option isn't available, you need to install the PhotoTools 2.0 demo located in the Software folder on the CD-ROM.) Click the Reset button to make sure you start at the same spot as this technique. (For all the PhotoButton steps in this technique, if I do not list a value for a specific setting, leave it at the default value.)

Here are the settings I used in the Shape tab: (Width: 90, Height: 90, Inner Height: 0, Bevel Height: 50, Bevel Width: 15, Bevel Curve: 50).

3 Click on the Color tab. Below the Color tab, you will see that the Inner tab is active. Here are the settings I used in the Inner tab: (Surface Reflectivity: 30, Diffuse Angle: 40, Highlight Ratio: 30). In the Bevel tab, I used: (Surface Reflectivity: 30, Diffuse Angle: 30, Highlight Ratio: 60). In the Outer tab, turn on the Transparent and

No Highlighting checkboxes. Click the Apply button.

4 Now we want to create the On button. Make the On layer active. Choose Filter➡PhotoTools➡ PhotoButton 2.0 again. When PhotoButton opens, it will display the settings we used last. Change the Inner Height to 100% and leave all the other settings alone.

5 Make the On layer invisible and make the Off layer active. Switch to default colors and create the text for the button. After you create and position the text, choose Layer➡Type➡Render Layer. This will convert the type layer into pixels so that we can apply filters to the text. Rename the type layer Label.

6 The text can be raised from the surface of the button by creating a fake emboss with layers. Duplicate the Label layer (Label copy). Fill the Label copy layer with white while preserving transparency by pressing (Cmd+Shift+Delete) [Ctrl+Shift+Backspace]. Set the blending modes of both the Label and Label copy layers to Soft Light. This will make the text temporarily disappear. Make the Label layer active. Select the Move tool and nudge the Label layer one pixel down by pressing the down arrow key on the keyboard once, and one pixel right by pressing the right arrow key on the keyboard once.

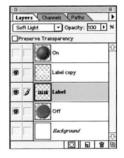

125

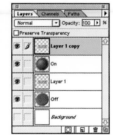

7 To further emphasize the text, duplicate the Layer copy layer (Layer copy 2). Make the Label layer active. (Cmd+click) [Ctrl+click] on the Label copy layer, then (Cmd+Shift+click) [Ctrl+Shift+click] on the Label layer to select the complete text outline. Choose Edit➡ Copy Merged. Choose Edit➡Paste. This will create a new composite layer (Layer 1) of the three layers you used to create the text effect. Delete the Label, Label copy and Label copy 2 layers.

8 Make the On layer visible. Duplicate the Layer 1 layer (Layer 1 copy) and move the layer above the On layer. (Cmd+click) [Ctrl+click] on the On layer to load a selection in the shape of the round button. Choose Select➡Modify➡Contract (6).

In the next step, you will be using the Spherize filter. The trick to using this filter correctly is to limit the area that the filter works on. Because the On button has a beveled border around it, we need to contract our selection to just inside this border so that the text won't expand into the bordered edge when we apply the Spherize filter.

9 Choose Filter➡Distort➡
Spherize (Amount: 65, Mode:
Normal). Deselect the selection.
Choose Layer➡Merge Down. Make
the Layer 1 layer active and Choose
Layer➡Merge Down. You now have
your on and off button states.

You can view these On and Off
buttons in action in a JavaScript
rollover by opening the sphere.htm
file located in the Animations folder
on the CD-ROM in a Web browser
such as Netscape Navigator or
Microsoft Internet Explorer. ●

Spherize

PART III

Edge Effects

Break images out of their boring rectangular boxes! The many techniques in this section of the book teach you how to create interesting image frame and border effects. Sometimes it is not enough to have pretty pictures on a page. At times, you need to draw more attention to an image by emphasizing its importance by adding a creative edge to it.

This section will have you making your photographs more interesting very quickly. As with many of the other techniques in this book, experimentating with the values for some of the steps will generate many variations.

This section of the book offers several techniques for manually creating interesting image frame and border effects with Photoshop. This particular technique shows you how to make professional-looking results with a few clicks of your mouse using a plug-in called PhotoFrame. A fully functional 30-day demo of this plug-in can be found in the Software folder on the CD-ROM. You should install the demo before following the steps in this technique.

1 Open the image to which you want to add a frame. If you want to follow along with this example, you can open the apples.psd file found in the Artwork folder on the CD-ROM.

130

TOOLBOX

PhotoFrame

2 Choose Filter➡Extensis➡ PhotoFrame. Click the Demo button. The first time you open PhotoFrame, the frame slots in the upper-left corner will be empty (Frame 1, Frame 2, Frame 3). Choose the frame file you want to use with your image.

3 Click the Add Frame button. In the Open dialog box, locate the following directories: (Hard drive/ Extensis PhotoFrame 1.0/Frame Files Vol.1 Sample) [C://Program Files/Extensis/ Extensis PhotoFrame 1.0/Frame Files Vol.1 Sample]. The demo installer includes 10 sample frame files to choose from, five from each volume. Volume 1 is Painted Edge Effects, Volume 2 is Digital Edge Effects. (There are more than 150 frames in each volume in the full version.) When you click on a frame name, you will see a thumbnail preview to make sure that it is the frame file you want to use. Choose the camera_02.frm file.

4 Once the frame file is loaded into PhotoFrame, you can interactively adjust any of the attributes for the Background or the Border of the frame, including size, rotation, position, blur, opacity, blend mode, and color. PhotoFrame has multiple undo/redo, so feel free to experiment with the settings. You will see any adjustments you make to the settings affect the preview window in real time. For this example, I went with the default settings.

5 When you like what you see, click the Apply button. PhotoFrame returns the image to Photoshop with its stylish new framed edge.

VARIATIONS

For this variation, I chose black for the Background color. Then I clicked on the Border tab and used Border Size: 2%, Blur: 2, and chose white for the Border color.

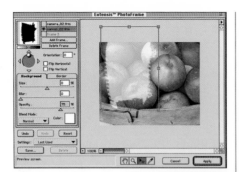

For this variation I hid the camera_02.frm frame by clicking off its eyeball in the upper-left corner list. I clicked the Add Frame button and chose the canvas_02.frm sample frame file. I resized the frame file to make it smaller, and positioned it partially off the edge of the image. I then inverted the frame file by clicking on the grayscale color ramp bar at the bottom of the thumbnail preview. Finally, I changed the Background Opacity to 75%.

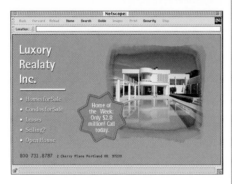

The framed house in the Web page example used the watercolor_08.frm sample file.

With this technique, you can make the edge of a photograph, or any object for that matter, look like it has been burned. The magic of this effect is the Clouds filter and a little tricky work with Curves.

1 Start with a photograph of your choice. If you would like to follow along using the example from the book, open the fog.psd file in the Artwork folder on the CD.

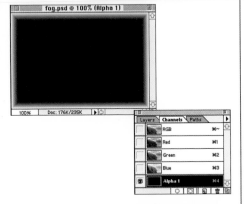

2 Select All. Choose Select➡Modify➡Border (15). Choose Select➡Save Selection. Deselect the selection and make the Alpha 1 channel active.

134

TOOLBOX

burnt_curve 01

burnt_curve 02

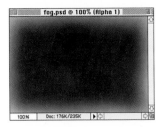

3 To create the burned edge, choose Filter➡Blur➡Gaussian Blur (Radius: 15). Choose Filter➡Render➡Clouds. Choose Filter➡Fade Clouds (Opacity: 40%, Mode: Normal). The clouds create a pattern that will eventually evolve into a ragged edge.

4 Choose Filter➡Blur➡Gaussian Blur (Radius: 4). Choose Image➡ Adjust➡Levels (Input Levels: 119, 1, 139). This extreme levels adjustment defines the edge and removes the unwanted grey pixels.

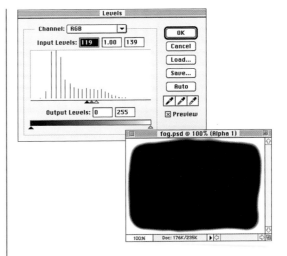

5 Choose Filter➡Blur➡Gaussian Blur (Radius: 15). Choose Filter➡ Fade Gaussian Blur (Opacity: 100%, Mode: Lighten).

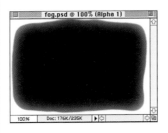

6 Create a new channel (Alpha 2) and choose Filter➡Render➡ Clouds. This new channel will be used to make a selection that will help modify the Alpha 1 channel later.

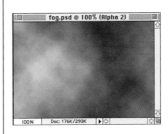

135

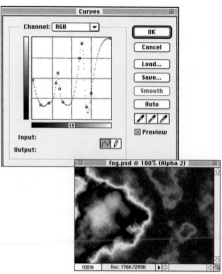

7 Choose Image➡Adjust➡Curves. Click the Load button and choose the burnt_curve_01 file from the Curves folder on the CD-ROM.

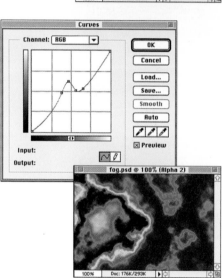

8 Choose Image➡Adjust➡Curves. Click the Load button and choose the burnt_curve_02 file from the Curves folder on the CD-ROM. These Curves adjustments to the clouds pattern are what really bring out the ragged, burnt edge look.

9 Make the Alpha 1 channel active. (Cmd+click) [Ctrl+click] on the Alpha 2 channel to load the Alpha 2 channel as a selection on the Alpha 1 channel.

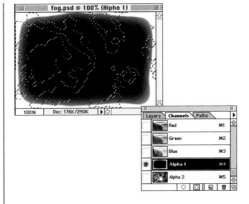

10 Choose Edit➥Fill (Use: White, Opacity: 50%, Mode: Normal, Preserve Transparency unchecked). Deselect the selection.

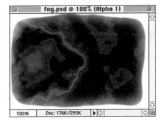

11 Choose Image➥Adjust➥Levels (Input Levels: 123, 1, 167).

12 Return to the composite channel. Press (Cmd+Option+4) [Ctrl+Alt+4] to load the Alpha 1 channel as a selection. Press (Delete) [Backspace] to delete the selection (the selection marquee will still be active after deleting).

137

13 Choose Select➡Feather (Radius: 15). Choose a foreground color (RGB: 97, 58, 9) and fill the selection twice while preserving transparency by pressing (Opt+Shift+Delete) [Alt+Shift+Backspace] two times. Feathering the selection and using the dark brown color is what makes the edge look like it has been held up to a flame.

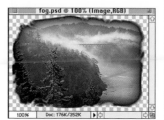

14 Press (Cmd+Option+4) [Ctrl+Alt+4] to reload the Alpha 1 channel as a selection. Choose Select➡Feather (Radius: 3). Switch to default colors and fill the selection with the foreground color (black) while preserving transparency twice (Opt+Shift+Delete) [Alt+Shift+Backspace]. Deselect the selection. Repeating the filling using black with a smaller feather radius is what creates the portion of the edge that was closest to the flame.

VARIATIONS

For this variation, I started with a layer filled with the color of the Web page. In Step 2, I used the Marquee tool and selected half the layer. Instead of choosing Select➡Border, I went straight to saving the selection as a channel. I used Gaussian Blur (Radius: 15) and then followed the rest of the steps.

Here is the burnt edge in action as a repeating background tile on a Web page.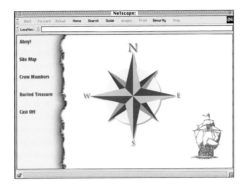

A popular way to make photographs more interesting is to break them out of their boring rectangular boxes and add a creative frame or edge around them. Photoshop has many built-in filters that you can use to make some cool edge effects—and don't stop with these! Once you've got the concept down, start experimenting on your own!

The Spatter Filter

1 Open any image to which you want to add an edge effect. Rename the layer that your image is on Image.

2 Create a new layer (Layer 1). Fill it with white (or whatever color the background of your Web page will be) and move Layer 1 below the Image layer.

3 Choose Image➡Canvas Size and increase the Width and Height to 110%. This gives you extra work space around the image for the edge effect.

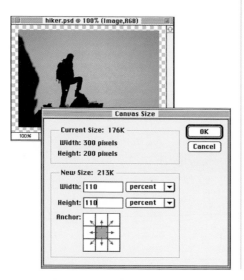

140

4 Make the Image layer active and choose Layer➡Add Layer Mask➡ Reveal All. Then (Cmd+click) [Ctrl+click] on Layer 1 to load a selection the size and shape of the original image dimensions. Choose Select➡Modify➡Contract (16).

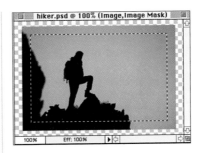

5 Invert the selection and fill it with white. Deselect the selection. You are now ready to apply a filter, or filters, to the layer mask on the Image layer to create the edge effect.

6 Choose Filter➡Brush Strokes➡Spatter. Experiment with the settings. I used Spray Radius: 12, Smoothness: 5. A large Spray Radius setting makes the edge effect wider. A large Smoothness setting makes the edge somewhat coarse.

141

7 You have been working on the layer mask of Layer 1; now you need to switch back to the image. Make the Image layer active then (Cmd+click) [Ctrl+click] on Layer 1 again to load a selection.

8 Choose Image➡Crop. This returns the canvas size to its original dimensions.

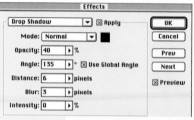

9 For the final touch, choose Layer➡Effects➡Drop Shadow (Mode: Normal, Color: Black, Opacity: 40%, Angle: 135, Distance: 6, Blur: 3, Intensity: 0). This adds a nice, soft drop shadow behind the image.

VARIATIONS

Spatter with (Spray Radius: 6, Smoothness: 1) and without a drop shadow layer effect.

Spatter with (Spray Radius: 20, Smoothness: 15).

The Sprayed Strokes Filter

I Follow all the steps of the Spatter Filter technique above, replacing Step 6 with the following:

Choose Filter➡Brush Strokes➡ Sprayed Strokes. Experiment with the settings. I used (Stroke Length: 10, Spray Radius: 6, Stroke Dir: Right Diagonal). The Stroke Length obviously determines how long the strokes will be. The Spray Radius determines how wide and how coarse the strokes will be.

Here is the final image after it has been cropped and had a drop shadow applied to it.

VARIATIONS

Sprayed Strokes with (Stroke Length: 20, Spray Radius: 20, Stroke Dir: Horizontal).

Sprayed Strokes with (Stroke Length: 10, Spray Radius: 15, Stroke Dir: Vertical).

143

The Torn Edges Filter

1 Follow Steps 1 through 5 of the Spatter Filter technique.

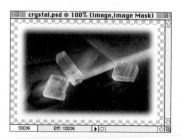

2 Choose Filter➡Blur➡Gaussian Blur (Radius: 5). The Torn Edges filter will give you better results if it has something to work with other than a straight hard edge. In this step you will try to blur the edge of the mask.

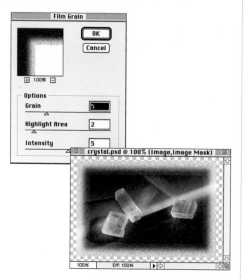

3 Choose Filter➡Artistic➡Film Grain (Grain: 5, Highlight Area: 2, Intensity: 5). This filter is similar to the Add Noise filter in that it adds random pixels to the image. In this case, I like it better than the Add Noise filter because it provides much more control. The grain will make the results of the Torn Edges filter more random.

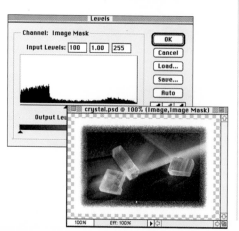

4 Choose Image➡Adjust➡Levels (Input Levels: 100, 1.00, 255). This helps define the edge by removing the excess grain and gray pixels outside the edge boundary.

5 Choose Filter➡Sketch➡Torn
Edges (Image Balance: 2,
Smoothness: 15, Contrast: 18). After
you're done with this step, continue
on from Step 7 in the Spatter Filter
technique above.

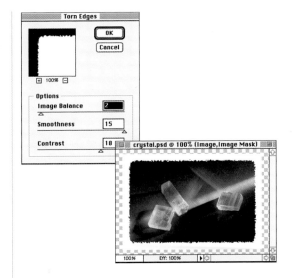

Here's the final image after it has
been cropped and had a drop shadow applied to it.

VARIATIONS

For a smoother edge, try the Torn
Edges filter with (Image Balance: 10,
Smoothness: 2, Contrast: 10) and
no drop shadow. ●

Slides

TOOLBOX

slide.psd

A common way to display images on a Web site is to provide a small thumbnail of the image that the user can click on if they want to see the larger image. The thumbnails are great for several reasons. They download quicker than full size images, and they give the user a choice—if they don't want to see the larger image, they don't have to click on the thumbnail. This technique demonstrates an interesting twist on the standard thumbnail by placing the small preview image inside a slide holder.

First, I scanned an actual slide holder on my normal desktop scanner. (Sorry, not very magical, but why waste time drawing a slide holder when you can just scan one?) Most people don't think to use their scanners for anything other than flat photographs, but you really can scan anything! If you can't close the lid completely, you'll want to cover the object with an opaque white sheet of paper or cloth.

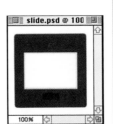

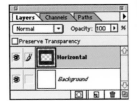

1 For this technique, I've made things even easier: You can just open the file I made, slide.psd, from the Artwork folder on the CD-ROM. (After I scanned the slide holder into Photoshop, I simply duplicated the Background layer and named the duplicate Horizontal. I filled the Background layer with white. On the Horizontal layer, I selected the background and the inside window of the slide with the Magic Wand tool and pressed (Delete) [Backspace].)

2 I want a row of four thumbnails so I need to resize the canvas to make more room for the additional slides. Switch to default colors. Choose Image➥Canvas Size. I chose Width: 600, Height: 200, Anchor: from the left-center.

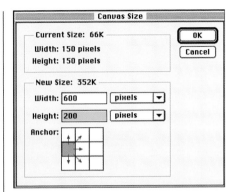

3 Duplicate the Horizontal layer three times. Rename the four slide layers One, Two, Three, and Four. Move the slides around in the image window so that they are not overlapping each other by choosing the Move tool, making the layer you want to move active, and pressing and dragging the slide around in the image window.

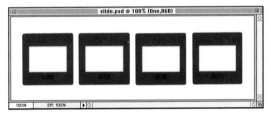

4 To add a little visual variety, I'm going to adjust the placement of some of the slide frames. Make the One layer active. Choose Edit➥ Transform➥Numeric (Rotate Angle: -10).

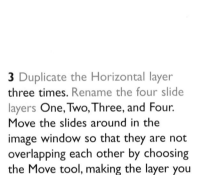

TIP **You will need to remember how much you rotated each slide so that you can rotate the photographs you drop into the slides the same amount.**

147

5 I want the third slide to hold a vertical picture instead of a horizontal picture. Make the Three layer active. Choose Edit➡Transform➡ Rotate 90° CW, then choose Edit➡Transform➡Numeric (Rotate Angle: -10).

6 Make the Four layer active. Choose Edit➡Transform➡Numeric (Rotate Angle: 5).

7 Rearrange the slides so that they are overlapping each other slightly. Once you like how they are arranged, hide the Background layer and choose Layer➡Merge Visible. Rename the merged layer **Slides**, and make the Background layer visible.

8 Choose Layer➡Effects➡Drop Shadow (Mode: Normal, Color: Black, Opacity: 50%, Angle 135°, Distance: 10, Blur: 8, Intensity: 0%).

9 Open a photograph that you want to use as a thumbnail. Choose Image➡Image Size. If you are using a horizontal photo, in Pixel Dimensions, change the Height to 70 pixels. If you are using a vertical photo, change the Height to 100 pixels.

10 Select the Move tool and drag the small photo into the Slide document. Make sure the photo layer is below the Slides layer. Choose Edit➡Transform➡Numeric and rotate the photo the same amount as the slide you want it to appear in, then position the photo exactly where you want it to appear within the slide.

11 Repeat Steps 7 and 8 for the other three photos you want to use.

This image could also make an interesting navigation bar—think of each slide as a button to another page and build an imagemap. ●

This edge effect gives your image that cool torn edge look you see with handmade papers.

I Open any image that you want to give an edge effect. Rename the layer Image.

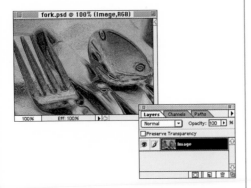

2 Create a new layer (Layer I). Fill it with black (or whatever color the background of your Web page will be) and move Layer I below the Image layer.

3 Choose Image➡Canvas Size and increase the Width and Height by 110%. This gives you a little extra room around the image for the edge effect.

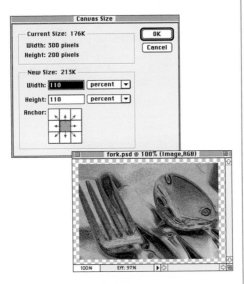

4 Make the Image layer active and choose Layer➡Add Layer Mask➡Reveal All. (Cmd+click) [Ctrl+click] on Layer I to load a selection the size and shape of the original image dimensions. Choose Select➡Modify➡Contract (12).

5 Inverse the selection and fill it with black. Deselect the selection. You are now ready to apply a filter or filters to the layer mask on the Image layer to create the edge effect.

6 Choose Filter➡Blur➡Gaussian Blur (Radius: 5).

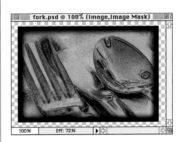

7 Choose Filter➡Sketch➡Chalk & Charcoal (Charcoal Area: 20, Chalk Area: 20, Stroke Pressure: 2). At this point, you could be done with the edge effect if you like the results. The rest of this technique describes how to brighten the edges a bit by adding highlight details. I think the extra polish really makes the hand-made paper edge come through.

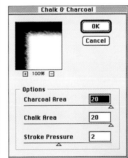

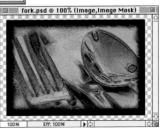

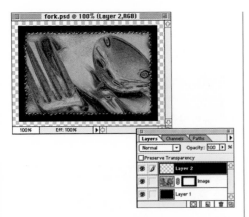

8 Create a new layer (Layer 2) and (Cmd+click) [Ctrl+click] on the Image layer mask to load a selection.

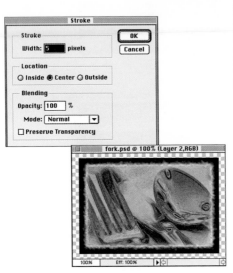

9 Switch to default colors and exchange the foreground and background colors so that white is the foreground color. Choose Edit➡Stroke (Width: 5, Location: Center, Opacity: 100%, Mode: Normal). Deselect the selection.

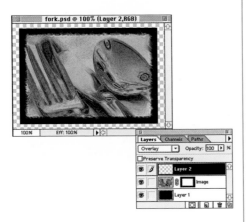

10 Set Layer 2's blending mode to Overlay.

11 (Cmd+click) [Ctrl+click] on Layer 1 to load a selection the shape and size of the original image dimensions.

12 Choose Image➡Crop. This returns the canvas size to its original dimensions. ●

zig-zag

You can use this technique to add a border effect to a photograph to call special attention to it on your Web page, or just to break an image out of its boring rectangular box.

1 Open the image you want to add a border effect to. Create a new layer and name it Temp. Switch to default colors and fill the Temp layer with the background color (white) by pressing (Cmd+Delete) [Ctrl+Backspace]. Choose Select➡All. Choose Select➡Modify➡Border (Width: 10). Select Image➡Adjust➡Invert or press (Cmd+I) [Ctrl+I]. Deselect the selection. This layer will be used several times to generate masks and selections in future steps.

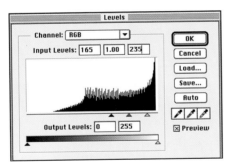

2 Choose Filter➡Blur➡Gaussian Blur (Radius: 40). Choose Image➡Adjust➡Levels (Input Levels: 165, 1.00, 235). This creates a wider border to manipulate in future steps.

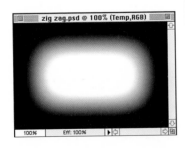

154

TOOLBOX

zig_zag_curve_01

zig_zag_curve_02

zig_zag_custom_01

3 Choose Edit➡Transform➡
Numeric and scale the Width and
Height 50%.

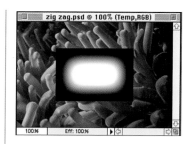

4 Before we can create the zig-zag
border, we need to fill in with black
the transparent area on the Temp
layer that was created by scaling
the layer in Step 3.

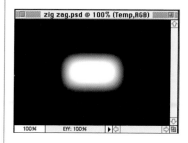

(Cmd+click) [Ctrl+click] on the
Temp layer to load the layer's trans-
parency mask as a selection.
Choose Select➡Inverse
(Cmd+Shift+I) [Ctrl+Shift+I] and fill
the selection with the foreground
color (black) by pressing
(Option+Delete) [Alt+Backspace].
Deselect the selection.

5 Choose Filter➡Distort➡Polar
Coordinates (Convert: Polar to
Rectangular). What the heck is the
Polar Coordinates filter doing? The
Polar Coordinates Rectangular to
Polar option shrinks the top edge
to a width of zero and puts it in
the middle of the image. Then, it
takes the bottom corners and
stretches them around and up until
they meet at the center of the top.
The Polar to Rectangular option
cuts a slit from the center of the
image to the top center, then drags
the two corners that it made down
to the lower corners of the image,
thus compressing the image into a
triangular area. Then it takes the
top of the triangle and stretches it
to the top corners of the image.
Therefore, the edges of the slit
together turn into the top edge of
the image.

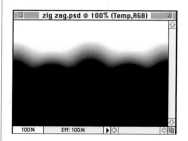

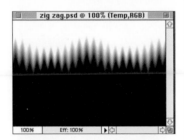

6 Choose Filter➟Distort➟Wave (Number of Generators: 1, Type: Sine, Min. Wavelength: 7, Max. Wavelength: 7, Min. Amplitude: 11, Max. Amplitude: 11, Horizontal Scale: 1%, Vertical Scale: 100%, Undefined Areas: Repeat Edge Pixels). This filter actually creates the zig-zag edge .

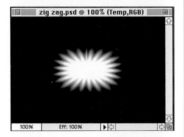

7 Choose Filter➟Distort➟Polar Coordinates (Convert: Rectangular to Polar). This puts the zig-zag edge back around a circular shape.

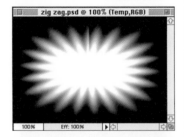

8 Choose Edit➟Transform➟ Numeric and scale the Width and Height 200% to return the mask to its original proportions.

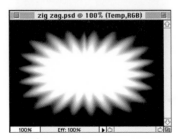

9 Choose Filter➟Blur➟Gaussian Blur (Radius: 1.5). Choose Image➟Adjust➟Levels (Input Levels: 35, 1.2, 235). This step gives the zig-zag a more clearly defined edge.

10 Duplicate the Temp layer and rename the layer **Temp: Border.** Make the Temp layer invisible. Choose Edit➡Adjust➡Curves. Click the Load button and locate the zig_zag_curve_01 file found in the Curves folder on the CD.

11 Choose Select➡Color Range (Fuzziness: 100). Click anywhere in the black area of the image window.

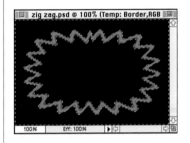

12 Press (Delete) [Backspace] to delete the selection and then deselect the selection.

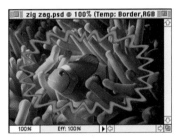

13 Choose a foreground color that you want to use for the border and choose Edit➡Fill (Use: Foreground Color, Opacity: 100%, Mode: Color, Preserve Transparency). Choose Layer➡Merge Visible. A great way to customize this border effect is to choose a color from within the image. To do so, select the Eyedropper tool and click on the color you want to use in the image before choosing Edit➡Fill.

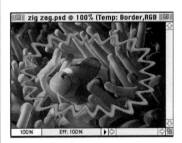

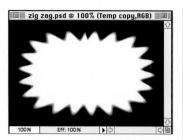

14 Duplicate the Temp layer (Temp copy). Choose Image➡Adjust➡ Levels (Input Levels: 15, 1.00, 100). You will use this layer to create a selection that will cut the bordered image out of its original background.

158

15 Choose Select➡Color Range (Fuzziness: 100) and click anywhere in the black area in the image window, then click OK. Delete the Temp copy layer. Choose Select➡Inverse.

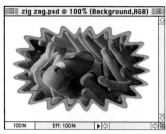

16 Choose Layer➡New➡Layer Via Copy or press (Cmd+J) [Ctrl+J] to create a new layer (Layer 1) that contains a copy of the selection. Rename Layer 1 Image. Make the Background layer active and fill it with the background color (white) by pressing {Cmd+Delete) [Ctrl+Backspace].

17 Double click on the Temp layer to open the Layer Options dialog box. Rename the Temp layer Highlights, set the Opacity to 70% and the Mode to Screen. Choose Layer➥Group with Previous or press (Cmd+G) [Ctrl+G].

18 For the final touches, we will add some highlight and shadow details.

Select Edit➥Adjust➥Curves. Click the Load button and locate the zig_zag_curve_02 file found in the Curves folder on the CD. Choose Filter➥Blur➥Gaussian Blur (Radius: 1). Choose Filter➥Other➥Custom. Click the Load button and locate the zig_zag_custom_01 file found in the Curves folder on the CD.

These curves and custom files work together to make the zig zag border look like it has depth, as if it were a raised plastic border.

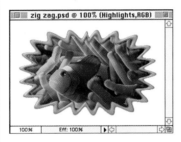

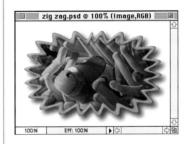

159

19 Choose Image➡Adjust➡Levels
(Input Levels: 0, .5, 200). Select
Filter➡Blur➡Gaussian Blur
(Radius: 1). Make the Image layer
active and choose Layer➡Effects➡
Drop Shadow (Mode: Normal,
Color: Black, Opacity: 70%, Angle:
135[deg], Distance: 10, Blur: 10,
Intensity: 0). ●

PART IV

Textures

Textures are fun to create and are often the building blocks of other effects. This section of the book teaches you how to create 11 specific textures. However, keep in mind that the techniques are often generic recipes, which means that with a little experimentation in the steps, you can create an endless number of variations of exciting textures.

The textures range from organic, natural looking images to synthetic and artificial ones. It is important to note that only some of the texture techniques described here result in "seamless" tiles where you can use the tile repeatedly and not see an edge. The seamless tiles are appropriate to use as background tiles for your Web pages. The other textures listed are often used for the type, button and animation techniques found throughout the rest of the book. You will find that the book often cross-references itself to further inspire you by showing you examples of how the textures can be used in real-life applications.

This Acid texture combines three different filters—the Add Noise, Motion Blur, and Difference Clouds filters—and is a spin off of a classic technique that creates wood grain and other organic textures.

1 Create a new document with dimensions large enough to use this texture with other elements. I used 200 × 200.

2 Choose a foreground color (I used RGB: 237, 145, 20) and fill the Background layer with it by pressing (Option+Delete) [Alt+Backspace].

3 Choose Filter➞Noise➞Add Noise (Amount: 80, Distribution: Gaussian, Monochromatic).

Add Noise dialog box — OK, Cancel, Preview; 100%; Amount: 80; Distribution: Uniform / Gaussian; Monochromatic.

4 To make the streaking rain, choose Filter➞Blur➞Motion Blur (Angle: 45°, Distance: 45). To bring out the streaks even more, run the Motion Blur filter two more times; (Cmd+Option+F) [Ctrl+Alt+F] reopens the last filter and shows you the settings that you used. Leave the angle set to 45°, but change the distance to 50 the second time and to 60 the third time.

As you can see, these first four steps are the basic ingredients that create a jumping-off point for endless variations of textures. To experiment you can apply any number of filters to this image—like Wave, Twirl, or Ripple from the Filter➡Distort submenu.

 Remember, don't be afraid to go off in a different direction. With Photoshop 5's History palette, it is quite simple to return to a previous point in your work if you don't like how your tangent turned out.

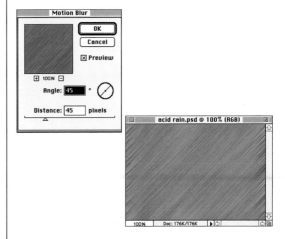

5 Now to add the acid rain clouds. Choose a foreground and background color. You will use the Difference Clouds filter multiple times, so it does not really matter what colors you choose. You can even change colors each time before using the filter. Choose Filter➡Render➡Difference Clouds.

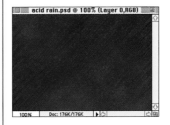

If your colors are similar in hue or darkness, your clouds will not have much contrast. For more contrast, try two colors that are at opposite ends of the spectrum, or a light and dark color.

6 Repeat the filter by pressing (Cmd+F) [Ctrl+F] until you like what you see. Be careful! This technique is addicting and mesmerizing; you might find it difficult to stop.

163

If you like the looks of the effect but want to apply the filter one more time just to try it out, save a copy of the image so you can come back to it later.

Here are some examples of this texture in use. To see how the button is created, turn to page 94. To see how the carved effect is created, turn to page 210. ●

Acid Rain

This is a great technique that creates a cloth texture like linen or burlap.

I Create a new document (300 × 200, Transparent). Switch to default colors. Fill Layer I with the foreground color (black) by pressing (Option+Delete) [Alt+Backspace].

2 Choose Filter➯Noise➯Add Noise (Amount: 400, Distribution: Gaussian, Monochromatic). The amount of noise determines how dense the weave of the cloth will be.

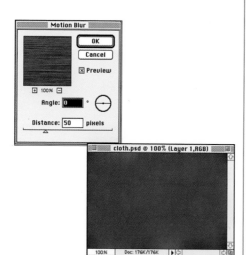

3 Choose Filter➯Blur➯Motion Blur (Angle: 0, Distance: 50). Choose Filter➯Blur➯Motion Blur again, or press (Cmd+Opt+F) [Ctrl+Alt+F] to reopen the Motion Blur filter (Angle: 90, Distance: 50). Using the Motion Blur filter twice with two different angles creates the weave pattern. It is best to stay with 90 degree increments, because other degree settings will create funky results.

4 Choose Filter➞Stylize➞Emboss (Angle: 135, Height: 3, Amount: 500). The Emboss filter will create the necessary depth so that the threads look like they are weaving in and out.

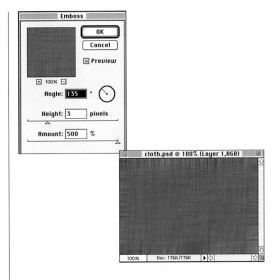

5 Choose Image➞Adjust➞Levels (Input Levels: 85, 1.00, 170). This extreme level adjustment finishes off the effect by increasing the contrast of the cloth pattern so that the individual threads become more defined.

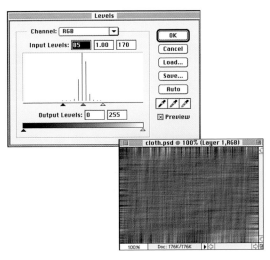

167

VARIATIONS

It is very easy to colorize this texture—just choose Image➞Adjust➞Hue/Saturation and turn on the Colorize check box.

For this variation of the cloth texture, I used (Hue: 230, Saturation: 30, Lightness: 0).

CLOTH

Textured Photographs

Another cool way to use any texture is to apply it to photographs. Just open an image you would like to apply a texture to and create a new layer (Layer 1). Create your texture on this new layer and set the Layer 1 blending mode to something other than Normal, such as Overlay.

Remember, different blending modes can alter the effect significantly. Here is the same image with the blending mode set to Screen.

Crumpled Paper

You can make your photograph appear to have been wadded up into a ball and then spread back out again if you use the Stone texture (page 196) and set the Layer 1 blending mode to Hard Light.

An Aged Mock Duotone

If you go a few steps beyond just applying a texture to a photograph, it is very easy to create a mock duotone effect as well.

For this example, I duplicated the original Image layer and chose Image➡Adjust➡Desaturate to turn the duplicate into a grayscale image without having to change the mode of the image. On another layer above the desaturated original, I created the Rust texture (page 190) and desaturated it as well. I set the blending mode for the Rust layer to Screen. Finally, I created one additional layer and filled it with a color (RGB: 153, 153, 102) and set its blending mode to Color.

You can use any texture you want in place of the Rust texture. (Note: you only have to desaturate the texture if it is not already a grayscale texture.) You can choose any color you want for the Color layer as well.

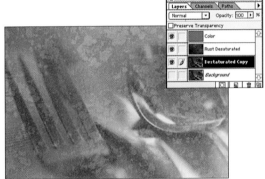

169

Here's a reminder that many of the techniques in this book can be combined to create new variations and interesting effects. In this particular example, I applied the cloth texture to a photograph and then used the Curled Page and Burnt Edge techniques. ●

This texture combines three different filters—Texturizer, Stained Glass, and Glowing Edges—in that order. With simple variations, you can create cobblestone, alligator, and lizard skin, or even tropical fish scales!

1 Create a new document with dimensions large enough to use this texture with other elements. I used 200 × 200.

2 Choose a foreground color (a blue hue like RGB: 50, 65, 185) and fill the Background layer with it (Option+Delete) [Alt+Backspace].

3 Choose Filter➡Texture➡ Texturizer (Texture: Burlap, Scaling: 100%, Relief: 4, Light Dir: Top). This filter adds a believable randomness to the surface of the stones.

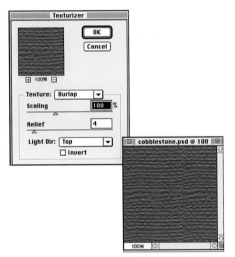

4 Switch to default colors. Choose Filter➡Texture➡Stained Glass (Cell Size: 10, Border Thickness: 2, Light Intensity: 4). Don't be surprised to see that the burlap texture you created in Step 3 has disappeared.

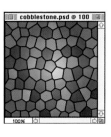

5 Choose Filter➡Fade Stained Glass (Cmd+Shift+F) [Ctrl+Shift+F]. The Fade command lists whichever filter was used last, as long as you choose the Fade command right after you run a filter. If you perform any other task immediately after applying a filter, you lose the opportunity to use the Fade command. The Fade dialog box also contains an Opacity slider. Lowering it reveals the original burlap texture through the stained glass texture. Set the Opacity to 50% and leave the Blend mode set to Normal.

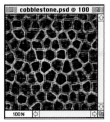

6 Choose Filter➡Stylize➡Glowing Edges (Edge Width: 2, Edge Brightness: 8, Smoothness: 4). Combined with the next step, Glowing Edges creates the "mortar" between your cobblestones.

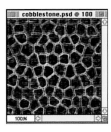
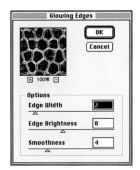

171

7 Again, when you apply the Glowing Edges filter, it completely eliminates the previous texture. Choose Filter➡Fade Glowing Edges (Cmd+Shift+F) [Ctrl+Shift+F]. Set Opacity to 20% and change the Blend mode to Difference.

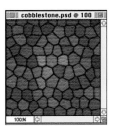

VARIATIONS

Alligator Skin

For this variation, I used a green fill, instead of blue, and used the Filter: Noise: Add Noise (Amount: 50, Distribution: Gaussian, Monochromatic). For Step 3, I used a Relief setting of 6. For Step 4, I used a Light Intensity setting of 6 and for Step 6, I used an Edge Brightness setting of 6. For Step 7, I chose an Opacity setting of 40% and set the mode to Normal.

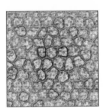

Goldfish

For your own bowl of fish, select Image➡Adjust➡Hue/Saturation (Hue: +160).

Snake Skin

On the other hand, if you run Filter➡Stylize➡Find Edges after Step 7, it turns into real snake skin. ●

You have seen this effect in video game graphics and in outer space movies where a low-quality video stream is displayed. This interlacing technique is created by transmitting only half the image, with every other line of the image alternating with a solid line of black. Follow the steps below to define the pattern you need to create this effect, or open the interlace_01.psd file from the Patterns folder on the CD-ROM and skip to Step 4.

1 Create a new document (100 × 50, transparent). Switch to default colors. Select the Single Row Marquee tool and click anywhere in the image. Zoom to 1600%.

2 Fill the selection with the foreground color (black). Move the selection marquee down so that it is adjacent to and below the black line you just created.

3 Fill the selection with the background color (white). Deselect the selection.

4 (Cmd+click) [Ctrl+click] on Layer 1 to select the two-line pattern. Choose Edit➡Define Pattern.

5 Open the image that you want to apply this effect to. If you want to follow along with the book, open the multi-glow.psd file from the Artwork folder on the CD-ROM.

6 Create a new layer (Layer 1). Choose Edit➡Fill (Use: Pattern, Opacity: 100%, Mode: Normal).

7 Set Layer 1's blending mode to Soft Light. Soft Light makes the white lines transparent so that the black lines appear to hide every other row of pixels.

VARIATIONS

Experiment with this effect by changing the blending mode of the Pattern layer and by adjusting the thickness of the lines in the pattern. Here I made the lines of the pattern 2 pixels tall instead of 1, and I chose Multiply for the blending mode.

Changing the blending mode to Overlay yields this result.

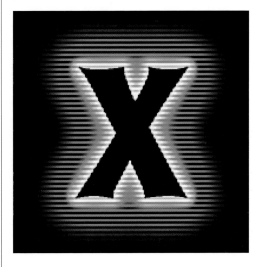

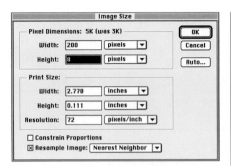

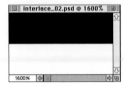

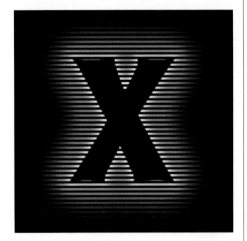

interlaced

TIP If you want to change the thickness of the lines, open the interlace_01.psd or interlace_02.psd file from the Patterns folder on the CD-ROM. You can use Image➡Image Size. Just turn off the Constrain Proportions check box and double the Height value in the Pixel Dimensions area. However, make sure that you choose Nearest Neighbor for the Resample option. If you leave it at the default setting of Bicubic, your lines will end up anti-aliased. You don't want any gray pixels in your lines, only black and white. (Nearest Neighbor will resize your artwork without anti-aliasing it.) After you have changed the size of the image, proceed to Step 4.

Here are some examples using other images.

To create this seersucker pattern for this button, I used two shades of blue instead of black and white when creating the pattern. After filling the layer with the pattern, I rotated the layer 30 degrees. (Edit➡Transform➡Numeric, Rotate Angle: 30°) ●

This texture is just plain fun to make. When you are finished, you will have a texture that looks like warm liquid plastic, kind of like boiling metallic fingernail polish. Don't be intimidated by the number of steps. As you will see, it is not an exact science, and you can eliminate or add steps as you see fit. The trick is to get comfortable with the Curves command.

1 Open the plastic.psd file from the Artwork folder on the CD-ROM. The tones in the image will define the shapes in the texture. The great thing about this technique is that it will generate a different texture every time if you use a different photograph (and the final result will look nothing like the contents of the image!) If you use your own image, make sure the mode is set to RGB. (Choose Image➡Mode➡RGB.)

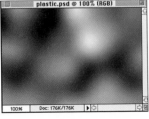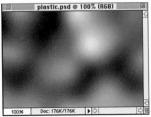

2 Choose Image➡Adjust➡ Desaturate to end up with a grayscale version of your image without changing the mode.

3 Choose Filter➡Blur➡Gaussian Blur (Radius: 10). Choose Image➡Adjust➡Auto Levels. Choose the Gaussian Blur filter again with a Radius of 12 (Cmd+Option+F) [Ctrl+Alt+F]. This step eliminates the details of the original photograph, turning it into soft blobs.

4 Choose Image➡Adjust➡Curves (Cmd+M) [Ctrl+M]. You can load the plastic_curve_01 file from the Curves folder on the CD-ROM, or to create a curve setting similar to the one shown here, choose the Pencil tool. Hold down the Shift key and click points on the grid to create a "W" shaped curve. To blend the transitions, click the Smooth button. It really doesn't matter what settings you choose—create some crazy curve until you like what you see.

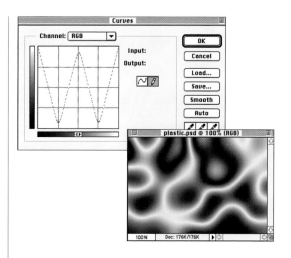

5 Choose Filter➡Blur➡ Gaussian Blur again (Radius: 2) (Cmd+Option+F) [Ctrl+Alt+F].

6 Choose Image➡Adjust➡Curves (Cmd+M) [Ctrl+M]. Create a curve like a "U" or load the plastic_curve_02 file from the Curves folder on the CD-ROM. This "U" shaped curve is how you can custom "solarize" any image. This technique gives the plastic its metallic shine.

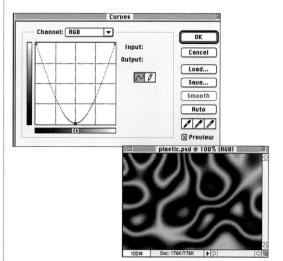

179

7 Duplicate the Background layer (Background copy) and set the layer blend mode to Difference. The image will appear as solid black at this point but don't worry, things will get interesting in the next step.

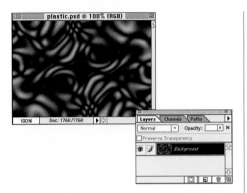

8 Choose Edit➡Transform➡Rotate 180°. Choose Layer➡Merge Down (Cmd+E) [Ctrl+E]. Combined with the blending mode change to Difference in Step 7, by duplicating and rotating the texture, it will begin to look psychedelic.

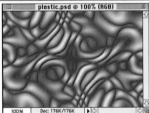

9 Choose Filter➡Other➡Custom and enter the values shown, or load the plastic_custom_01 file. The Custom filter performs a convolution on the brightness values in the image. That's pretty technical! It adds a sense of depth to your texture and lightens the image overall.

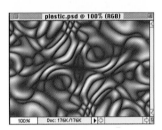

10 Choose Image➡Adjust➡Auto Levels. Choose Filter➡Fade Auto Levels (Opacity: 25%, Mode: Normal). Feel free to experiment with your own settings. Different mode settings can create interesting variations.

11 Choose Image➥Adjust➥
Hue/Saturation (Cmd+U) [Ctrl+U].
Turn on the Colorize check box.
Adjust the Hue, Saturation, and
Lightness sliders until you've col-
orized your liquid plastic to the
desired effect. (I used Hue: 360,
Saturation: 45, Lightness: 0.)

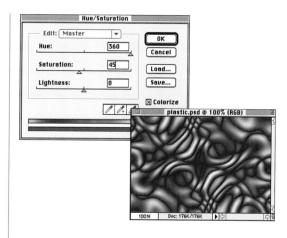

VARIATIONS

Using different colors can significantly change the mood of the texture.

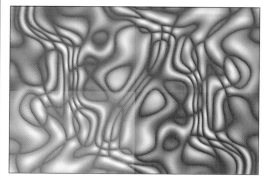

You can use this texture on
buttons...

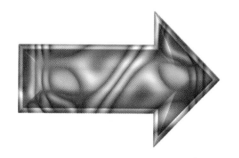

...or as the background texture for
carved type (see page 210) ●

181

Drawing a repeating field of dots could be a challenge using just the Marquee tool. Here is an easy way to create a field of perfect circles in Photoshop, a.k.a. polka dots.

1 Create a new document with appropriate dimensions for a background tile, usually no larger than 100 × 100 pixels. In order for this to be used as a seamless background tile for a Web page, the tile size you choose needs to be able to be divided by 5 or 10 evenly.

2 Double-click the name of the Background layer and rename it Layer 1. Choose a foreground and background color. Fill Layer 1 with the background color (Cmd + Delete) [Ctrl + Backspace].

3 Create a new layer (Layer 2) and fill it with the foreground color (Option + Delete) [Ctrl + Backspace].

4 Add a layer mask to Layer 2. Choose Edit➡Fill (Shift + Delete) [Shift + Backspace]. Use 50% gray for the contents, Opacity: 100%, Mode: Normal.

5 Make sure that the layer mask for Layer 2 is active; then choose Filter➡Pixelate➡Color Halftone. If you create a background tile, set the Max. Radius to the size of your image divided by 5 or 10; I used 20. If you are going to use this texture for anything other than a seamless tile, the number you choose does not matter.

Choose zero for the Screen Angles for all the channels.

6 Create a new layer (Layer 3) above Layer 2. Hold down the (Option) [Alt] key, then choose Layer➡Merge Visible. Alternatively, you can use this complex but wonderful keyboard shortcut (Cmd + Option + Shift + E) [Ctrl + Alt + Shift + E]. Like I always say, when in doubt, just hold down the entire left-hand side of your keyboard.

This merges a copy of the visible layers (Layer 1 and Layer 2 into Layer 3), creating a composite layer but leaving you with the individual layers still intact for future editing.

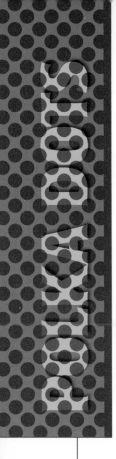

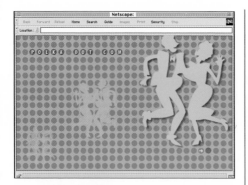

VARIATIONS

Adding Text

Using Clipping groups, it is very
easy to create this variation. After
you have created the tile and filled
a layer with it, duplicate this layer.
Create a text layer in-between the
two polka dot texture layers.
Choose Image➡Adjust➡
Hue/Saturation, turn on the
Colorize box, and change the color
of the top texture layer. To make
the top texture layer appear only
in the text, choose Layer➡Group
with Previous (Cmd+G)
[Ctrl+G]. ●

This is a great technique that creates recycled paper using the Pointillize filter in to recreate the little shards of colored paper you can see in recycled paper.

1 Create a new document (300 × 200, Transparent). Switch to default colors. Choose a foreground color (RGB: 222, 207, 170). Fill Layer 1 with the foreground color by pressing (Option+Delete) [Alt+Backspace].

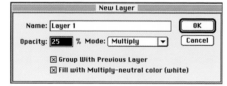

2 Choose Layer→New→Layer (Opacity: 25%, Mode: Multiply, Group With Previous Layer, Fill with Multiply-neutral color). Certain Photoshop filters, like Lighting Effects and Pointillize, will not work on empty layers (layers that don't contain pixels). Selecting the Fill with Neutral Color option when creating a new layer allows you apply these filters to empty layers by filling the layer with a preset neutral color. Until you do something else to this new layer, your image won't look any different on screen.

3 Choose Filter→Pixelate→Pointillize (Cell Size: 10). This will sprinkle the bits and pieces of recycled paper into the image. It is also a great way to make confetti! The cell size determines the size of the shards. If you want more chunkier paper, use a bigger number.

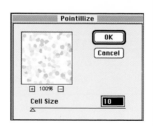

4 Choose Filter→Stylize→Find Edges. This defines the shapes of the shards a bit more.

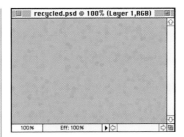

5 Choose Filter→Artistic→Dry Brush (Brush Size: 2, Brush Detail: 8, Texture: 1). This will shred the little bits and pieces of paper to make them look more realistic. Brush Size determines the density and Brush Detail determines the raggedness of the shards.

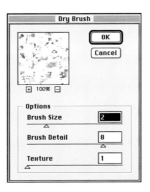

6 Choose Layer→Merge Down (Cmd+E) [Ctrl+E]. For the final touch, choose Filter→Noise→Add Noise (Amount: 5, Distribution: Gaussian, Monochromatic). This adds a slight grain to the paper making it look more realistic.

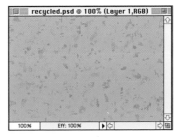

187

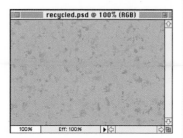

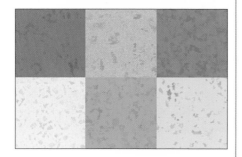

VARIATIONS

It is easy to end up with lots of different paper types here with different colors and texture. You can choose different colors in Step 1, adjust the opacity setting in Step 2, and adjust the values you use in Steps 3, 5 and 6.

Remember the Curled Page Button technique? (If not, then turn to page 104 to check it out.) Well, now you can be politically correct and use only stock that contains 20% post consumer waste for your onscreen graphics. ●

This is a great technique that produces realistic rusted metal. The Grain and Dry Brush filters create a weathered look.

1 Create a new document (300 × 200, white). Choose a foreground color (RGB: 112, 45, 7) and a background color (RGB: 44, 20, 70). Select Filter➡Render➡Clouds.

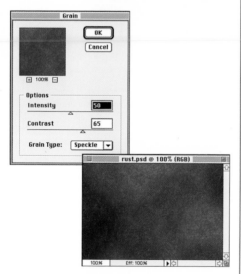

2 Choose Filter➡Texture➡Grain (Intensity: 50, Contrast: 65, Grain Type: Speckle). Rusted metal usually has a gritty, flaky surface. This filter starts the rust aging process.

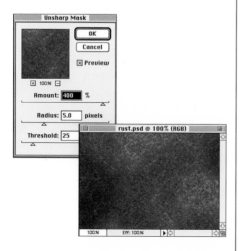

3 Choose Filter➡Sharpen➡ Unsharp Mask (Amount: 400, Radius: 5, Threshold: 25). This will increase the contrast and define edges throughout the rusted surface.

4 Choose Filter➡Artistic➡Dry Brush (Brush Size: 2, Brush Detail: 2, Texture: 2). This filter provides the magic needed to pull off this texture. The Dry Brush filter will smooth out the dark and light portions of the image while leaving flaky edges between high contrast areas.

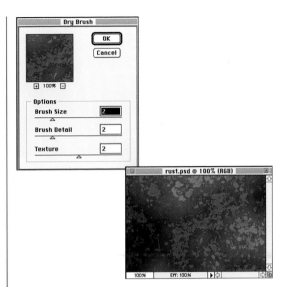

5 Choose Filter➡Noise➡Add Noise (Amount: 12, Distribution: Gaussian, Monochromatic).

VARIATIONS

To create these double-beveled buttons, I made rectangular selections and used a plug-in called Extensis PhotoBevel. PhotoBevel is part of a collection of seven different plug-ins in PhotoTools 2.0. Good news! You can find a fully functional, freeware version of this plug-in on the book CD-ROM in the Software folder. It is yours to use and keep. To learn how to make many different bevel effects, turn to page 100.

The text was created with the Carve technique found on page 210.

By changing a few of the steps, it is easy to create a patina finish. Metalworkers create a patina finish by giving metal an acid bath and firing it with a blowtorch. In Step 1, I chose a foreground color (RGB: 237, 135, 81) and a background color (RGB: 160, 76, 48) and then ran the Clouds filter. Then, I switched to default colors and selected Filter➡Render➡ Difference Clouds. I skipped Step 2 and followed the other steps.

I used this texture when I created these round buttons with the technique found on page 94. ●

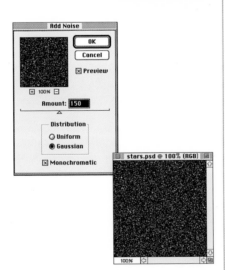

Have you ever wished you could make your own private universe? The following technique is an insanely fast way to generate a star field.

I Create a new document with appropriate dimensions for a background tile, usually no larger than 100 × 100 pixels. Because there will only be a few shades of gray in the final tile, the file size of this tile will be very small. Therefore, you can use larger dimensions if you want.

2 Switch to default colors. Fill the Background layer with black (Option+Delete) [Alt+Backspace].

3 Choose Filter➡Noise➡Add Noise (Gaussian, Monochromatic). The amount you choose determines how dense your star field will be. I used 150, but you determine how many stars exist in your universe. Add more noise than you think you need because, depending on what you do in Step 5, 60 to 90 percent of the noise you see here disappears.

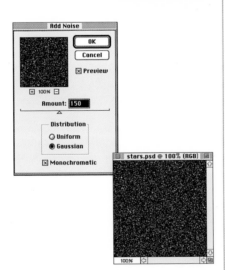

194

4 Choose Filter➡Blur➡Gaussian Blur. The more you blur, the more variation you have in individual star sizes. I chose a Blur Radius of 0.5.

5 Now for the fun part. Choose Image➡Adjust➡Levels. You will want to play with the three Input triangles to adjust how your star field looks. Make sure that the Preview check box is turned on so that you can see the adjustments you make.

There is no real technical explanation here; just slide the triangles around until it looks right to you. I usually slide the black triangle quite a bit to the right and the white triangle quite a bit to the left and then play with the gray triangle until I like what I see. When you are happy, click the OK button. ●

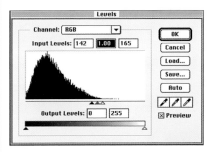

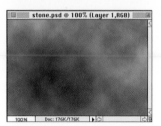

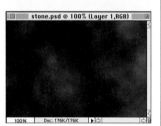

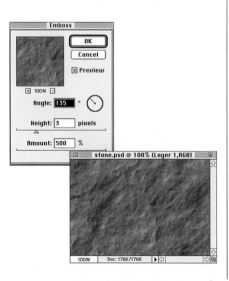

This is a great technique that creates a very realistic stone or slate texture.

1 Create a new document (300 × 200, Transparent). Switch to default colors. Fill Layer 1 with the foreground color (black) by pressing (Option+Delete) [Alt+Backspace].

2 Choose Filter➥Render➥Clouds. If you hold down the Shift key as you choose the Clouds filter, you will end up with a clouds texture with more contrast. A higher contrast will result in deeper pits and steeper peaks on the surface of the stone.

3 Optional step: Choose Filter➥ Render➥Difference Clouds. If you use only the Clouds filter, you will end up with a smoother surface. Adding the Difference Clouds to the effect will intersperse random ridges and indentations. (I used Difference Clouds in this example.)

4 Choose Filter➥Stylize➥Emboss and play with the settings until you are happy with the stone texture. I used (Angle: 135, Height: 3, Amount: 500).

VARIATIONS

It is very easy to colorize this texture. Just choose Image➡Adjust➡ Hue/Saturation and turn on the Colorize check box.

For this variation of the cloth texture, I used (Hue: 60, Saturation: 35, Lightness: -5).

Here is an example of the stone texture being used in a Web page as the background element of an interactive button bar. ●

You learned how to create a star field texture in the Stars technique that you used as a background tile or as source material for text or graphics. The star field can also be used as the foundation to create a complete background image of an alternate universe.

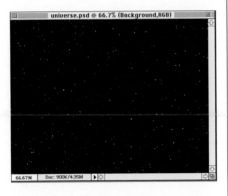

1 Create a new document the size of your Web page—in this case, 640 ×480—and repeat Steps 2 through 5 on page 194 to create the star texture.

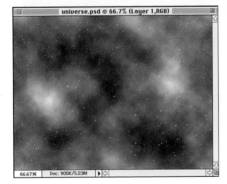

2 We now want to add clouds across the middle of our universe. Switch to default colors. Create a new layer (Layer 1) and choose Filter➤Render➤Clouds. Set the layer's Blending Mode to Screen, which ignores all the black pixels in Layer 1 to reveal the stars from the Background layer through the clouds.

3 We want the clouds to take on a gaseous look. Change the foreground color to these RGB values: 176, 0, 0. Experiment with other colors if you want to. Choose Filter➡Render➡Difference Clouds and you end up with some toxic-looking colors. This is the step where you can really have some fun. Repeat the last filter (Cmd + F) [Ctrl + F] as many times as you want to customize the space clouds. You can even choose different foreground colors before repeating the Difference Clouds filter.

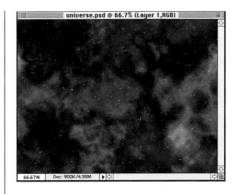

4 Add a layer mask to Layer 1. Paint on the layer mask with the Paintbrush tool (start with a 35-pixel soft-edged brush and experiment) to hide portions of the clouds you do not wish to see. If you hide too much and wish to reveal portions of the clouds again, simply switch the foreground and background colors and paint back over the hidden areas.

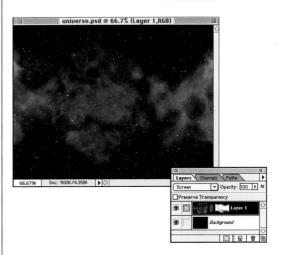

5 For the final touch, add a bright star or sun to your universe. Switch to default colors. Create a new layer (Layer 2), fill it with black (Option + Delete) [Alt + Backspace], and set the layer blend mode to Screen. When you are finished with this step, the image appears unchanged from Step 4. Again, by setting the layer Blend mode to screen, you are telling Photoshop to ignore any black pixels on that layer.

6 Choose Filter➡Render➡Lens Flare. You don't get a very large preview to work with, but play around with the Brightness, Flare Center, and Lens Type until you are happy with the star. Be careful not to make the brightness too high or you wash out your composite image. When you like what you see, click the OK button.

You can reposition the star if you want to by moving the layer around the image with the Move tool. Also, if you want to adjust the strength of the clouds, adjust the opacity of Layer 1.

Here is an example of how this image could be used as a back-ground for a Web page. ●

PART V

Type Effects

Now that Web designers have ways to ensure that the viewer sees their pages using the fonts the page was originally designed with, it is less necessary to create text blocks as graphics. This section of the book concentrates on creative display text effects that can be used to add character to a Web page.

As an added bonus, two of the effects, Bricks and Multi-Glow, also appear in the Animations section of the book as animated variations of the static text effects. You can find demos of these animations on the CD.

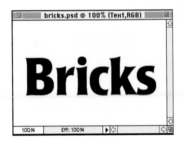

This technique will show you how to build your text out of bricks. You could use this technique to create an interesting rollover effect by having a pile of bricks on your Web page. When the visitor moved his or her mouse over the pile, it could turn into a word or phrase built out of bricks.

1 Create a new document (Contents: White) with dimensions large enough to have plenty of space around the text so that it isn't accidentally trimmed. Create black text. The text will end up on its own layer above the Background layer. Choose Layer➡Merge Down (Cmd+E) [Ctrl+E] to merge the text layer with the Background layer. Rename the Background layer to Text.

This Text layer will be a source layer that you will duplicate many times to create the various parts of this technique.

2 Create a new layer and name it Background. Switch to default colors and fill the Background layer with the background color (white) by pressing (Cmd+Delete) [Ctrl+Backspace].

This Background layer represents the background of your Web page. If your page will use a color other than white, fill the Background with the color you plan on using.

TOOLBOX

bricks_01.psd

3 Create a new layer and name it Mortar. Choose a foreground color (RGB: 50, 0 , 0). Move the Mortar layer above the Background layer. Fill the Mortar layer with the foreground color by pressing (Opt+Delete) [Alt+Backspace].

4 Duplicate the Text layer (Text copy). Move the Text copy layer above the Mortar layer. Choose Filter➡Blur➡Gaussian Blur (Radius: 3).

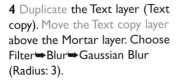

5 Choose Filter➧Stylize➧Emboss (Angle: 135, Height: 3, Amount: 90).

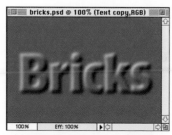

6 Set the Text copy layer's blending mode to Hard Light. Choose Layer➧Merge Down (Cmd+E) [Ctrl+E].

7 Duplicate the Text layer (**Text copy**). Move the Text copy layer above the Mortar layer. Choose Filter➥Blur➥Gaussian Blur (Radius: 3). This is only a temporary layer that you will use to derive a selection.

8 Choose Image➥Adjust➥Levels (Input Levels: 43, 1.00, 192). This Levels adjustment helps define the black-and-white areas and eliminates extra gray pixels so that you can derive a clean selection in the next step.

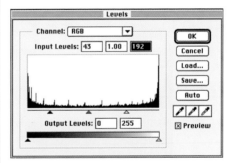

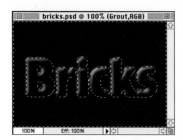

9 Choose Select➡Color Range. Set the Fuzziness to 72 and click anywhere in the image preview other than on the letters. This instantly selects all the white pixels in the Text copy layer.

10 Delete the Text copy layer. (You should have an active selection marquee on the Mortar layer at this point).

11 Press (Delete) [Backspace] to delete the non-text pixels on the Mortar layer. Deselect the selection.

12 Create a new layer and name it Bricks. Choose a foreground color (RGB: 150, 0 , 0) and a background color (RGB: 223, 178, 178). Select Filter➡Render➡Clouds. This Bricks layer is the layer that will actually have the bricks on it. The Clouds filter with these colors creates the color and surface of the bricks.

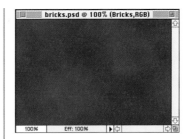

13 Duplicate the Text layer (**Text copy**). Move the Text copy layer above the Bricks layer. Set the Text copy layer's blending mode to Hard Light.

14 Open the bricks_01.psd file from the Patterns folder on the CD. Select all and choose Edit➡Define Pattern. Close the bricks_01.psd file.

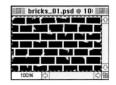

15 Choose Edit➡Fill (Contents: Pattern, Opacity: 100%, Mode: Lighten).

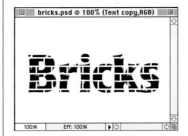

207

16 Choose Filter➡Blur➡Gaussian Blur (Radius: 2). Choose Edit➡Blur➡Gaussian Blur again (Radius: 4). Choose Filter➡Fade Gaussian Blur (Opacity: 65%, Mode: Lighten).

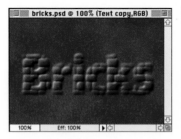

17 Choose Filter➡Stylize➡Emboss (Angle: 130, Height: 2, Amount: 130). Choose Layer➡Merge Down (Cmd+E) [Ctrl+E].

18 Duplicate the Text layer (Text copy). Move the Text copy layer above the Bricks layer. Choose Edit➡Fill (Contents: Pattern, Opacity: 100%, Mode: Lighten).

19 Select Filter➡Blur➡Gaussian Blur (Radius: 1.5). Choose Select➡Color Range. Set the Fuzziness to 72 and click anywhere in the image preview other than on the letters. As before, Color Range quickly makes a selection for you.

20 Delete the Text copy layer. (You should have an active selection marquee on the Bricks layer at this point). Press (Delete) [Backspace] to delete the non-text pixels on the Bricks layer. Deselect the selection.

21 Make the Mortar layer active. (Cmd+click) [Ctrl+click] on the Bricks layer. Choose Layer➡Add Layer Mask➡Reveal Selection. This is an important step because it makes the technique look more like the letters were created by stacking the bricks on top of each other. Without the layer mask, the technique looks like the letters were cut out of a brick background texture.

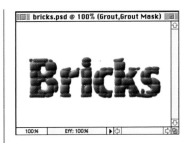

22 This last step is optional if you want to add a drop shadow to the effect. Make the Bricks layer active. Select Layer➡Effects➡Drop Shadow (Mode: Normal, Opacity: 100%, Angle: 135°, Distance: 2, Blur: 5, Intensity: 0). ●

This technique shows you how to create text that looks as though it has been carved into a background texture, complete with highlights and shadows for realistic depth. As you can see in the variations, this can be used on objects besides text.

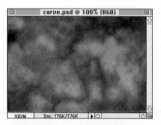

1 Start with a texture or background of your choice. If you would like to follow along using the example from the book, open the "carve.psd" file from the Artwork folder on the CD-ROM.

2 Choose white as the foreground color. Create the text.

3 Duplicate the Background layer (Background copy) and rename the layer "Carve Fill." Adjust the opacity of the Carve Fill layer to 80%. Move the Carve Fill layer above the text layer and choose Layer➡Group with Previous (Cmd+G) [Ctrl+G].

4 Create a new layer and rename it Shadow. Switch to default colors and fill the Shadow layer with the foreground color (Option+Delete) [Alt+Backspace].

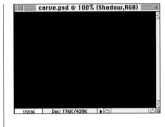 

5 (Cmd+click) [Ctrl+Click] on the text layer. (You should see the cursor change to the index finger with the Marquee tool while you are holding the (Cmd) [Ctrl] key down.) This creates a selection in the shape of the text on the Shadow layer.

6 Fill the selection with the background color (white) and deselect the selection.

7 Choose Filter➡Other➡Offset (Horizontal: 4, Vertical: 4, Repeat Edge Pixels).

8 Choose Filter➡Blur➡Gaussian Blur (Radius: 4). The Offset and the Gaussian Blur create the drop shadow detail and the photo-realistic depth.

211

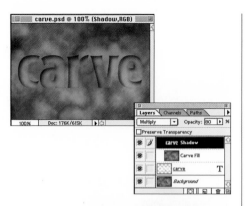

9 Choose Layer➡Group with Previous (Cmd+G) [Ctrl+G]. Adjust the opacity of the Shadow layer to 80% and set the blending mode to Multiply.

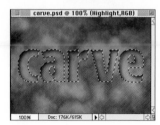

10 Create a new layer and rename it Highlight. (Cmd+click) [Ctrl+Click] on the text layer to create a selection of the text on the Highlight layer.

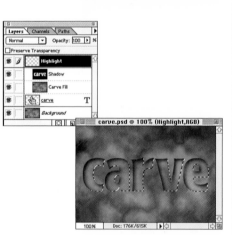

11 Choose the Marquee tool. Nudge the selection one pixel down and one pixel to the right. (Cmd+Option+click) [Ctrl+Alt+Click] on the text layer. This will subtract the original text selection from the selection you just moved, leaving you a sliver of a selection to create the carve highlight.

12 Fill the selection with the background color **(white)** and deselect the selection. Set the blending mode of the Highlight layer to Overlay.

What makes this particular method of creating this carved or cutout effect really cool and flexible is the fact that the text can be repositioned at anytime. To do so, link the Shadow, Highlight, and text layers before using the Move tool.

VARIATIONS

In addition to text, this technique can also be used with simple line art drawings as well! Just create your artwork on its own layer with a transparent background and create the texture you want to carve the line art out of in its own layer.

I used this technique to make a fun set of buttons for a children's Web site about animals. ●

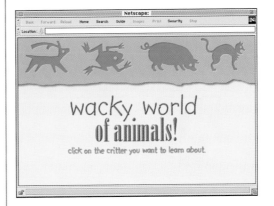

Multi-Glow

Have you ever wondered how they create the cool multi-colored glowing text that displays at the beginning of the *X-Files* television program? This technique teaches you how to re-create the effect as a static image. At the end of this technique, you will have the source file you need to re-create the effect as an animated image. The steps for the animated technique can be found starting on page 44.

1 Create a new document with dimensions large enough to fit the text. You want to create ample room for the glow to spread out comfortably without running into the edge of the image. Feel free to make the canvas size larger than you think you will need; you can always crop it down later. I used 200 × 200.

2 Switch to default colors. Fill the Background layer with black by pressing (Option+Delete) [Alt+Backspace].

3 Create the text. For now, in the Type Tool dialog box, choose white for the text color so you can see it against the black Background layer, and position the text in the center of the image.

4 Choose Layer➡Type➡Render Layer to convert the text to pixels. Rename the layer Text.

 You cannot apply filters and other pixel-level modifications to type layers in Photoshop 5. When you choose Render Layer, you are converting the type layer into a layer that can be modified by filters.

5 To create the inside glow, duplicate the Text layer (Text copy) and rename it White. Move the White layer below the Text layer.

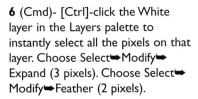

6 (Cmd)- [Ctrl]-click the White layer in the Layers palette to instantly select all the pixels on that layer. Choose Select➡Modify➡Expand (3 pixels). Choose Select➡Modify➡Feather (2 pixels).

7 Fill the selection with white (Cmd+Delete) [Ctrl+Backspace] and then deselect the selection.

 215

8 To create the middle glow, duplicate the White layer (White copy) and rename it Yellow. Move the Yellow layer below the White layer.

9 (Cmd)- [Ctrl]-click the Yellow layer in the Layers palette to instantly select all the pixels on that layer. Choose Select➡Modify➡Expand (3 pixels). Choose Select➡Modify➡Feather (3 pixels). Choose a yellow-green foreground color (RGB: 200, 255, 0) and fill the selection with it (Option+Delete) [Alt+Backspace]. Deselect the selection.

10 To create the outside glow, duplicate the Yellow layer (Yellow copy) and rename it Green. Move the Green layer below the Yellow layer.

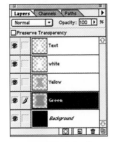

11 (Cmd)- [Ctrl]-click the Green layer in the Layers palette to instantly select all the pixels on that layer. Choose Select➡Modify➡Expand (6). Choose Select➡Modify➡Feather (10). Choose a green foreground color (RGB: 0, 255, 0) and fill the selection with it (Option+Delete) [Alt+Backspace]. Deselect the selection.

12 Select the Text layer. Switch to default colors. Fill the Text layer with the foreground color (black) while preserving transparency by pressing (Option+Shift+Delete) [Alt+Shift+Backspace].

There you have it! To see how to animate this technique, turn to page 44. ●

This technique will fill your type with water! You will end up with a block of text that is transparent so that you can see any texture or background image you want through the water.

1 Create a new document (Contents: White) with dimensions large enough to hold your text with plenty of space around it. Rename the Background layer Texture and create your background texture, image, or color there.

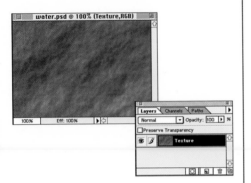

2 Create a new layer (Layer 1). Switch to default colors and fill the layer with the background color (white) by pressing (Cmd+Delete) [Ctrl+Delete]. Create the text and be sure to leave a generous amount of space around it so that it isn't accidentally trimmed. The text will end up on its own layer above Layer 1. Choose Layer➡Merge Down (Cmd+E) [Ctrl+E] to merge the Text layer with the white Layer 1. Rename the layer Text.

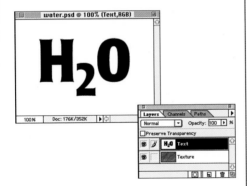

3 Make the Text layer active. Select all. Choose Edit➡Copy. Create a new channel (Alpha 1). Make the Alpha 1 channel active and choose Edit➡Paste. Deselect the selection.

4 Choose Filter➡Blur➡Gaussian Blur (Radius: 4). Choose Image➡Adjust➡Levels (Input Levels: 211, 1, 230). This will start to transform the letters into water forms by rounding the letters and spreading them out so that they are melding into each other.

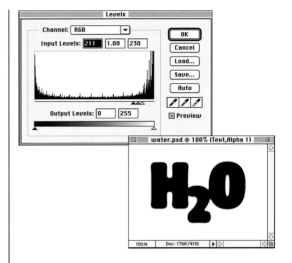

5 Return to the composite channel. Make the Text layer active. Select all and press (Delete) [Backspace]. Set the Text layer's blending mode to Hard Light.

6 Press (Cmd+Option+4) [Ctrl+Alt+4) to load the Alpha 1 channel as a selection. Invert the selection.

7 Choose Edit➡Fill (Use: Black, Opacity: 60%, Mode: Normal). Deselect the selection.

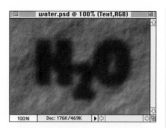

8 Choose Filter➡Blur➡Gaussian Blur (Radius: 5). Choose Filter➡Other➡Offset (Horizontal: 6, Vertical: 6, Repeat Edge Pixels). This step, combined with Step 9, will create the shadow that the raised water letter forms will cast onto the background.

9 Press (Cmd+Option+4) [Ctrl+Alt+4] to load the Alpha 1 channel as a selection. Invert the selection. Press (Delete) [Backspace] and then deselect the selection.

10 Create a new layer (Layer 1). Press (Cmd+Option+4) [Ctrl+Alt+4] to load the Alpha 1 channel as a selection. Invert the selection. Choose Edit➡Fill (Use: White, Opacity: 75%, Mode: Normal). Deselect the selection. Steps 10 through 12 create the physical water letter forms.

11 Choose Filter➡Blur➡Gaussian Blur (Radius: 8). Choose Filter➡Other➡Offset (Horizontal: -5, Vertical: -5, Repeat Edge Pixels).

12 Press (Cmd+Option+4) [Ctrl+Alt+4) to load the Alpha 1 channel as a selection. Press (Delete) [Backspace] and deselect the selection. Choose Layer➡ Merge Down.

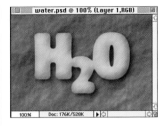 

13 Create a new layer (Layer 1). Press (Cmd+Option+4) [Ctrl+Alt+4) to load the Alpha 1 channel as a selection. Choose Edit➡Fill (Use: Black, Opacity: 70%, Mode: Normal). Deselect the selection. Steps 13 through 15 create the shadow detail on the water letter forms.

14 Choose Filter➡Blur➡Gaussian Blur (Radius: 7). Choose Filter➡ Other➡Offset (Horizontal: 8, Vertical: 5, Repeat Edge Pixels).

15 Press (Cmd+Option+4) [Ctrl+Alt+4) to load the Alpha 1 channel as a selection. Press (Delete) [Backspace] and then deselect the selection. Choose Layer➡Merge Down.

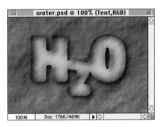 

16 Make the Alpha 1 channel active. Choose Filter➡ Blur➡ Gaussian Blur (Radius: 4). Choose Image➡Adjust➡Levels (Input Levels: 17, 1, 19). Choose Filter➡ Blur➡Gaussian Blur (Radius: 3). Steps 16 through 18 modify the Alpha 1 channel to create a mask that will be used to generate the highlight details of the water letter forms.

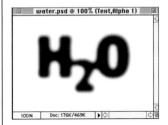 

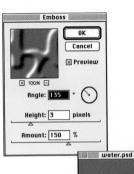

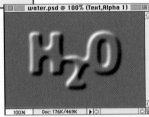

17 Choose Filter➡Stylize➡Emboss (Angle: 135, Height: 3, Amount: 150). The Emboss filter provides the photo-realistic height of the water.

18 Choose Image➡Adjust➡Levels (Input Levels: 198, .5, 250). This extreme Levels adjustment leaves us with just the highlight detail in the mask.

19 Return to the composite channel. Make the Text layer active. Press (Cmd+Option+4) [Ctrl+Alt+4) to load the Alpha 1 channel as a selection.

20 Choose Edit➡Fill (Use: White, Opacity: 90%, Mode: Normal). Deselect the selection.

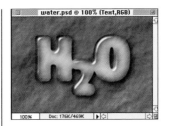

VARIATIONS

Again, what makes this technique very cool is the fact that the text is now transparent. Changing the color of the texture or replacing the texture altogether with a different image illustrates this. ●

Appendix A

Contributors Listing

The following companies have provided the software, filters, and stock photography for the CD-ROM that is included with this book. For more information on their products, use the contact information listed here.

Software

Extensis Corporation
1800 SW First Avenue Suite 500
Portland, OR 97201-5322
voice: 503/274-2020
fax: 503/274-0530
Web: http://extensis.com

Intellihance 3.0
MaskPro 1.0
PageTools 2.0
PhotoAnimator 1.0
PhotoBevel Solo 1.0
PhotoTools 2.0

Adobe Systems Incorporated
345 Park Avenue
San Jose, CA 95110-2704
voice: 408/536-6000
fax: 408/537-6000
Web: http://www.adobe.com

After Effects 3.1
Illustrator 7.0
ImageReady 1.0
PageMaker 6.5
PageMill 2.0
Photoshop 5.0
Streamline 4.0

Andromeda Software
699 Hampshire Road, Suite 109
Westlake Village
Thousand Oaks, CA 91361
voice: 805/379-4109, 800/547-0055
fax: 805/379-5253
email: andromeda@aol.com

Series 1: Photography Filters
Series 2: 3D Filters
Series 3: Screen Filters
Series 4: Techtures Filters
Shadow Filter
Velociraptor

Macromedia, Incorporated
600 Townsend Street
San Francisco, CA 94103
voice: 415/252-2000
fax: 415/626-0554
Web: http://macromedia.com

Acrobat Reader
Authorware
Director 6.5
Dreamweaver 1.0
Fireworks 3.0
Flash 3.0
FreeHand 8.0
Shockwave

Photoshop 5 Web Magic

Images

Photosphere Stock Images
380 West 1st Avenue
Vancouver, BC V5Y3T7
voice: 604/876-3206
fax: 604/876-1182
Web: http://photsphere.com

Appendix B

What's on the CD-ROM?

The CD-ROM included with this book is full of filters, images, and software applications for you to try. It is also where you will find the special preset files to be used with the effects described in this book.

The CD-ROM that comes with this book is both Macintosh and Windows CD-ROM compatible. Please note: There are several demos and tryouts available for Macintosh users that are not available for Windows users, and vice versa. This means one of two things: either the product has not been created for that platform, or a version of the product is being created but is not yet completed.

I suggest that you refer to the READ ME and other information files which are included in each demo program's folder. Also, visit the corporate Web sites; the URLs are noted in the Contributors Listing (Appendix A). There are often updated demos available for downloading and tryout.

Lighting FX Styles

Inside the Lighting FX Styles folder you will find two Lighting Style presets to be used with Photoshop's Lighting Effects filter. Proper installation of these files is critical. In order to use these files, they must be copied from the CD-ROM into the Lighting Styles folder within the Adobe Photoshop folder on your hard drive. Follow this path to find the proper folder: Adobe Photoshop 5.0➡Plug-ins➡Filters➡Lighting Styles. After copying these files, the next time you start Photoshop they will appear in the Style list in the Lighting Effects dialog box.

Artwork

The Artwork folder contains a variety of template images and stock art that are used in the techniques. To access these, you can open them directly from the CD, or copy them to your computer's hard drive and then work with them.

Animations

The Animations folder contains sample animations for the techniques on pages 26 through 92. Drag the file icons onto your Web browser window or open the file through your Web browser to see these. If you copy these files to your hard drive, be sure to copy the GIFs folder as well, because the graphics files used in the animations are stored there.

227

Curves

The files in the Curves folder contain information that Photoshop's Curves dialog box accesses to manipulate the images. You can open these files directly from the CD, or copy them onto your hard drive. In the Curves dialog box, click Load and navigate to the location where the file is stored and click OK.

Patterns

The pattern templates are sample files used to build repeating patterns. The files can be opened from the CD or copied to your hard drive.

Software

Inside this folder are demo versions of popular software applications that you can try. For detailed information about how to install and run these applications, consult the READ ME files that are contained within the individual folders. Each folder contains an installation file that walks you through the installation of the software.

Images

Inside the Images folder are a variety of low, medium, and high resolution stock photography images. Many of the images contain textures and backgrounds that can be used to make great-looking type. Most likely you will decide to keep these images on the CD, where you can access them at will—without having them eat up memory on your hard drive. (If you wish, they also may be moved to your hard drive.) All of these images can be opened with the Open command in Adobe Photoshop.

Gallery

Animations

page 34

page 42

page 44

page 54

Applications

Buttons

page 100

page 104

page 108

page 112

Edge Effects

Textures

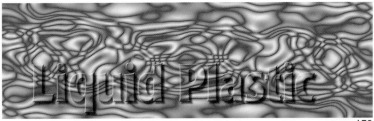

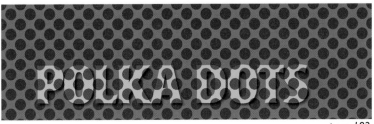

Type Effects

page 202

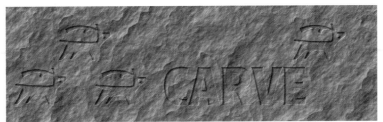

page 210

page 214

page 218

<deconstructing web graphics.2>

Web Design Case Studies and Tutorials

Deconstructing Web Graphics.2 profiles top web designers and programmers in order to demystify and analyze how they make decisions, solve complex issues, and create exceptional web sites. Adding her own voice and digital design teaching experience to the book, best-selling authors Lynda Weinman and Jon Warren Lentz select from their list of favorite designed web sites. They walk you through how to read and understand the source code for each page, break down all of the technical elements, and describe the inside details straight from the designers and programmers who created the pages.

This conversational and information-rich guide offers insight into web design that is not found through any other means. Profiles of successful web designers, programmers, photographers, and illustrators allow them to share their tips, techniques, and recommendations. You'll bring your own web design skills to a higher level through studying their experiences and the step-by-step tutorials and examples found in *Deconstructing Web Graphics.2*.

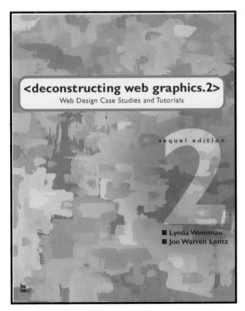

In this book, you'll learn about:

- Low-bandwidth graphics
- Scanned imagery for the web
- Cross-platform colors
- Custom Photoshop brushes and patterns
- Artwork using ASCII
- Copyright issues
- Animated GIFs
- LOWSRC animation tricks
- Tables for alignment
- Invisible GIFs for spacers
- Frames for navigation
- HTML tricks and workarounds
- Java
- JavaScript
- CGI
- Forms processing
- Server push
- Client pull
- Shockwave and Macromedia Director
- Sound and video files
- VRML

Product and Sales Information

Deconstructing Web Graphics by Lynda Weinman and Jon Warren Lentz
ISBN:1-56205-859-2 ▪ $39.99/USA ▪ 240 pages
Available at your local bookstore or online
Macmillan Publishing ▪ 1-800-428-5331
- http://www.lynda.com
- http://www.mcp.com/newriders

<coloring web graphics.2>
Master Color and Image File Formats for the Web

The purpose of this book is to help artists, programmers, and hobbyists understand how to work with color and image file formats for web delivery. Web browsers and different operating systems handle color in specific ways that many web designers aren't aware of. This updated second edition includes information about Photoshop 4.0, Illustrator 7.0, DitherBox, and DeBabelizer Pro.

A color palette of 216 browser-safe colors is identified and organized to help web designers confidently select successful cross-platform color choices and combinations. The book includes sections on color theory and understanding web color file formats, as well as step-by-step tutorials that explain how to work with browser-safe colors in Photoshop 4.0, Paint Shop Pro, Photo-Paint, Painter, FreeHand, and Illustrator 7.0. The cross-platform CD-ROM includes hundreds of suggested color combinations for web page design, as well as hundreds of palettes and browser-safe clip art files.

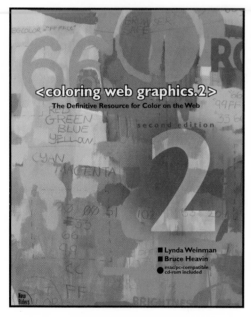

In this book, you'll learn about:

- Creating colors in your artwork that won't shift or dither across multiple platforms
- Choosing web-appropriate color schemes for your page designs
- Creating browser-safe hybrid variations
- Using Photoshop, Paint Shop Pro, Photo-Paint, FreeHand, Illustrator, and Director to manage web-specific color

The cross-platform CD-ROM includes:

- Browser-safe color palettes
- Browser-safe color swatches for Photoshop and other imaging programs
- Browser-safe colors organized by hue, value, and saturation
- Browser-safe color clip art for web use
- Electronic versions of color swatches grouped as they are in the book
- Sample HTML pages with recommended color groupings
- Sample patterns, backgrounds, buttons, and rules

Product and Sales Information

Coloring Web Graphics.2
By Lynda Weinman & Bruce Heavin
ISBN:1-56205-818-5 ▪ $50.00/USA ▪ 314 pages
Available at your local bookstore or online
Macmillan Publishing ▪ 1-800-428-5331
- http://www.lynda.com
- http://www.mcp.com/newriders

<designing web graphics.2>
How to Prepare Media and Images for the Web

Completely updated and expanded to include the latest on file formats, file sizes, compression methods, cross-platform web color, and browser-specific tehcniques, *Designing Web Graphics.2* is the definitive graphics guide for all web designers. If you are already working in the digital arts, in print or video, looking to transfer your skills to the web, this is the book for you. Step-by-step instruction in a conversational and easy to read style from a fellow artist/designer will help you understand the best methods and techniques for preparing graphics and media for the web.

Written in a conversational and user-friendly tone, *Designing Web Graphics.2* has received rave reviews from both experienced web designers and newcomers to the field. It's the bestselling book on this subject and is being used by web designers all over the world, including those from Hot Wired, Adobe, and Discovery Online.

In this book, you'll learn about:

■ Creating small and fast web graphics
■ Browser-safe colors for cross-platform use
■ GIFs, JPEGs, and PNGs through the use of comparison charts that help you pick the best compression method
■ Scanning tips (Photoshop 4.0 techniques)
■ Sound, animation, and interactivity
■ Creating navigation bars, rollover effects, and linked graphics
■ Step-by-step tutorials for programming Photoshop 4.0 action palettes
■ Practical applications for JavaScript, Shockwave, CGI, and plug-ins
■ Embedding inline music, animation, and movie files
■ Animated GIF creation techniques (how to control size, speed, and color palettes)
■ Creating GIF and PNG transparencies for the web
■ Web TV specs and authoring tips
■ Updated typography section

Product and Sales Information

Designing Web Graphics.2 by Lynda Weinman
ISBN:1-56205-715-4 ▪ $55.00/USA ▪ 500 pages
Available at your local bookstore or online
Macmillan Publishing ▪ 1-800-428-5331
■ http://www.lynda.com
■ http://www.mcp.com/newriders

<creative html design>

A Hands-On HTML 4.0 Web Design Tutorial

It's easy to make web pages with today's new WYSIWYG editors, but those programs don't teach you how to make fast-loading graphics, write accurate HTML that will endure for future browsers, or the necessary techniques involved in preparing your site for the web. Written by two of the industry's foremost experts, this definitive tutorial teaches you not just how to make a web page, but how to design web sites that are cross-platform compatible and work effectively within the web's distinct constraints.

Creative HTML Design walks you through all the phases of site design—from selecting an ISP and uploading files, to more advanced techniques like adding animation and rollovers. Step-by-step tutorials for Photoshop 4.0 and Paint Shop Pro teach how to design using "safe" colors, make distinctive background tiles, align your graphics, use tables and frames, include JavaScript rollovers, use CSS, as well as numerous other design and HTML features.

In this book, you'll learn about:

- How to build a finished web site with real-world examples and exercises
- How to write and read HTML
- Choosing an Internet service provider or presence provider
- Creating speedy GIF, JPEG, and PNG files
- Working with safe, cross-platform colors that will not shift in web browsers
- Designing distinctive background tiles, with and without visible seams
- Typographic principles and type tricks for the web
- Cascading Style Sheets
- Creating artwork and code for JavaScript rollovers
- Using tables to align text and graphics
- How to use frames aesthetically and effectively
- Using forms aesthetically so they fit the look of the rest of your site
- Adding animation and sound
- Organizing your pages on a server using relative URLs and SSI
- Troubleshooting automatically generated WYSIWYG HTML
- A complete HTML 4.0 reference

Product and Sales Information

Creative HTML Design
By Lynda Wienman and William E. Weinman
ISBN: 1-56205-704.9 ▪ $39.99/USA ▪ 434 pages
Available at your local bookstore or online
Macmillan Publishing ▪ 1-800-428-5331
- http://wwwcgibook.com
- http://www.mcp.com/newriders

The cross-platform CD-ROM includes:

- All the necessary files for the tutorials in this book
- JavaScript rollover code and many other customizable scripts

HTML Artistry: More Than Code

by Ardith Ibañez and Natalie Zee

HTML Artistry: More Than Code combines the latest and most popular uses of HTML 4 along with practical, real-world design advice to help you achieve sophisticated page layouts through the use of innovative typography, animation, and interactive effects that work on both Netscape Navigator and Microsoft Internet Explorer.

Authors and professional Web designers, Ardith Ibañez and Natalie Zee, make knowing what's hot in the Web design industry their top priority. Their discoveries will keep your sites on the cutting-edge of technology and will catch the eyes of everyone.

This hands-on, full-color, Web design guide clearly illustrates all aspects of HTML design, from the simple table layout to full animation with Dynamic HTML. Case studies and inspirational design models will teach you a variety of design principles and how to apply them to your site design. *HTML Artistry: More Than Code* will inform and inspire you to create innovative cross-browser Web sites.

Ardith Ibañez has designed Web sites and Web content for Macromedia, Sony Pictures Entertainment, California Pizza Kitchen, PhotoDisc, and MGM.

Her studio, Akimbo Design, has created work on the forefront of dynamic HTML Web site development, and Hewlett-Packard recently featured Akimbo in a commercial for their innovative use of computer technology. Ardith has also co-authored *HTML Web Magic* and *Creating Killer Interactive Web Sites*, both from Hayden Books.

Natalie Zee is a Web designer whose work can be seen on such Web sites as Macromedia, Visa, RankIt, Dynamic HTML Zone, and Student Advantage. She was awarded the 1997 Communication Arts Interactive Design Award for "Best Business Web Site" for her work on Macromedia's Web site.

Natalie is also the co-author of *HTML Web Magic* from Hayden Books.

ISBN: 1-56830-454-4   **$40.00 USA/$56.95 CAN**

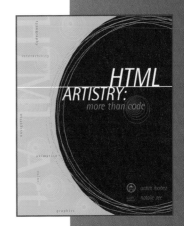

Inside Adobe Photoshop 5

by Gary Bouton, Barbara Bouton, Gary Kubicek

You can master the power of the world's most popular computer graphics program! Easy-to-follow tutorials, in Gary's famous style, teach you the full spectrum of Photoshop's powerful capabilities. The most comprehensive book available on Photoshop 5!

ISBN: 1-56205-884-3   **$44.99 USA/$63.95 CAN**

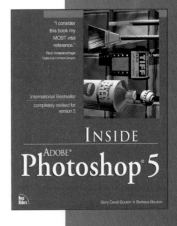

Dynamic HTML Web Magic

by Jeff Rouyer

Explore innovative DHTML techniques that you can combine, tweak, and apply to your own pages to create stunning designs and graphics. With step-by-step instructions, full-color illustrations, and the popular recipe-style Magic format, you'll be inspired with new artistic and technological know-how.

ISBN: 1-56830-421-8   **$39.99 USA/$56.95 CAN**

Click Here

by Raymond Pirouz

Written by an award-winning Web site designer, Click Here presents an expert's unique point of view on successful Web design, and teaches through hands-on tutorials how to think about, and implement, these designs. Topics covered inlcude: color, file size limitations, animation, load time, looping restrictions, and how to use popular design tools such as Photoshop, Illustrator, and GIFBuilder.

ISBN: 1-56205-792-8   **$45.00 USA/$63.95 CAN**

Photoshop 5 Type Magic

by Greg Simsic

This is the perfect resource for typographers, designers, and Photoshop users looking to spice up their work. Every page makes a visual promise: you will be able to create this exciting artwork! The book's highly effective, recipe-style approach walks you through the procedures of creating special effects with type, and the stunning four-color illustrations are sure to inspire any designer.

ISBN: 1-56830-465-X   **$39.99 USA/$56.95 CAN**

Photoshop Web Magic, Volume 1

by Ted Schulman, Renée LeWinter, and Tom Emmanuelides

This 4-color book provides numerous examples of dazzling Web graphics, textures, backgrounds, buttons, and animations in a recipe format with simple step-by-step instructions. Specific graphic techniques for customizing Web design to fit client needs and expert advice for print designers moving to the Web is included.

ISBN: 1-56830-314-9   **$45.00 USA/$63.95 CAN**

Photoshop Web Magic, Volume 2

by Jeff Foster

This companion volume to Photoshop Web Magic, Volume 1, includes 45 all-new techniques and provides step-by-step directions to create dazzling effects for the Web. A new section covers Java rollovers, animation tools, and WYSIWYG HTML editors.

ISBN: 1-56830-392-0   **$45.00 USA/$63.95 CAN**

Photoshop Magic Premier Collection

Save over $50 on five of the most popular Magic books and get *The Complete Guide to Photoshop Native Filters*—complete coverage of all 97 of Photoshop's filters—and a poster showing the effects of all of them.

The boxed set includes *Photoshop Web Magic, Photoshop Type Magic 1, Photoshop Type Magic 2, Photoshop Effects Magic,* and *Photoshop Textures Magic*. It's the perfect way to achieve special effects for the Web, create amazing type treatments, design stunning graphics and illustrations, and appkly eye-catching textures.

ISBN: 1-56830-442-0   **$149.99 USA/$214.95 CAN**

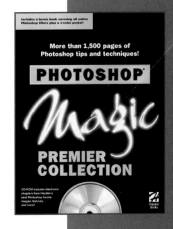

Illustrator Type Magic

by Greg Simsic

Every page of *Illustrator Type Magic* makes a visual promise: you will be able to create this! The book's highly effective, recipe-style approach walks you through the procedures of creating special effects with type, and the stunning four-color illustrations are sure to inspire any designer.

ISBN: 1-56830-334-3   **$39.99 USA/$56.95 CAN**

Fine Art Photoshop

by Michael Nolan

Create expressive artistic effects and polish your individual style with *Fine Art Photoshop*. Learn digital art techniques to make your work more original and intuitive—without third-party programs or filters. These simple exercises, practical examples, and step-by-step lessons helpyou master Photoshop and unleash your imagination and creativity. Based on traditional art instruction techniques, *Fine Art Photoshop* is like having your own painting class—in one book.

ISBN: 1-56205-829-0   **$39.99 USA/$56.95 CAN**

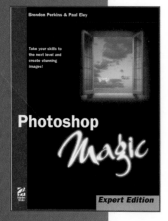

Photoshop Magic: Expert Edition

by Brendon Perkins

Photoshop Magic: Expert Edition takes you on an inspiration journey through the ins and outs of creating stunning, sophisticated expert effects—quickly and easily. This results-oriented guide unveils the secrets to enhancing your Photoshop skills and improving your performance.

Using a visually rich, step-by-step approach and the creative vision and technical expertise of Brendon Perkins, this authoritative guide illustrates every technique—photomontage, lighting effects, animations, and more—using masks, channels, layers, and advanced filters. You'll have all the tools you need to unleash your creativity!

ISBN: 1-56830-416-1   **$45.00 USA/$63.95 CAN**

Photoshop Channel Chops

by David Biedny, Nathan Moody, and Bert Monroy

Only true masters of Photoshop like these authors can unleash the power of channel operations. This book reveals the secrets they have used to create special effects for movies such as *Terminator 2: Judgment Day, Forrest Gump,* and more. *Photoshop Channel Chops* is a serious, practical guide to employing alpha channels, advanced masking techniques, interchannel mathematics, and a creative use of layers. Expert authors teach professional-level techniques for creating high-quality artwork worthy of print, CD-ROM, broadcast, and the Web.

ISBN: 1-56205-723-5   **$39.99 USA/$56.95 CAN**

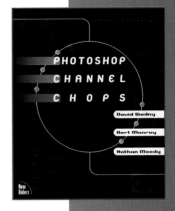

Sams Teach Yourself Adobe Photoshop 5 in 24 Hours

by Carla Rose

A fast tutorial for people new to Photoshop or looking for a quick introduction to the new features of Photoshop 5. In just 24 sessions of one hour or less, you will be up and running!

ISBN: 0-672-31301-4   **$19.99 USA/$28.95 CAN**

Using Adobe Photoshop 5

by Dan Giordan and Steve Moniz

A task-based reference that puts the answers to professionals' problems at their fingertips. Learn to create stunning graphics, correct and enhance tonality and focus of your images, and achieve professional results quickly with concise, step-by-step directions.

ISBN: 0-7897-1656-9   **$29.99 USA/$42.95 CAN**

Sams Teach Yourself Adobe Photoshop 5 in 21 Days

by T. Michael Clark

In just three weeks, you'll understand the fundamentals of Photoshop 5, master professional imaging techniques, learn how to effectively use all the tools and features, and get tips on creating spectacular designs quickly and easily. Using the step-by-step approach of this easy-to-understand guide, you'll be up to speed with Photoshop 5—in no time!

ISBN: 0-672-31300-6   **$39.99 USA/$56.95 CAN**

To order, visit our Web site at www.mcp.com or fax us at

1-800-835-3202

ISBN	Quantity	Description of Item	Unit Cost	Total Cost
1-56205-859-2		Deconstructing Web Graphics	$39.99	
1-56205-818-5		Coloring Web Graphics.2	$50.00	
1-56205-715-4		Designing Web Graphics.2	$55.00	
1-56205-704-9		Creative HTML Design	$39.99	
1-56830-454-4		HTML Artistry: More Than Code	$40.00	
1-56205-884-3		Inside Adobe Photoshop 5	$44.99	
1-56830-421-8		Dynamic HTML Web Magic	$39.99	
1-56205-792-8		Click Here	$45.00	
1-56830-465-X		Photoshop 5 Type Magic	$39.99	
1-56830-314-9		Photoshop Web Magic, Volume 1	$45.00	
1-56830-392-0		Photoshop Web Magic, Volume 2	$45.00	
1-56830-442-0		Photoshop Magic Premier Collection	$149.99	
1-56830-334-3		Illustrator Type Magic	$39.99	
1-56205-829-0		Fine Art Photoshop	$39.99	
1-56830-416-1		Photoshop Magic Expert Edition	$45.00	
1-56205-723-5		Photoshop Channel Chops	$39.99	
0-672-31301-4		Sams Teach Yourself Adobe Photoshop 5 in 24 Hours	$19.99	
0-7897-1656-9		Using Adobe Photoshop 5	$29.99	
0-672-31300-6		Sams Teach Yourself Adobe Photoshop 5 in 21 Days	$39.99	
		Shipping and Handling: See information below.		
		TOTAL		

Shipping and Handling

Standard	$5.00
2nd Day	$10.00
Next Day	$17.50
International	$40.00

201 W. 103rd Street, Indianapolis, Indiana 46290   1-800-835-3202 — FAX

Book ISBN 1-56205-913-0